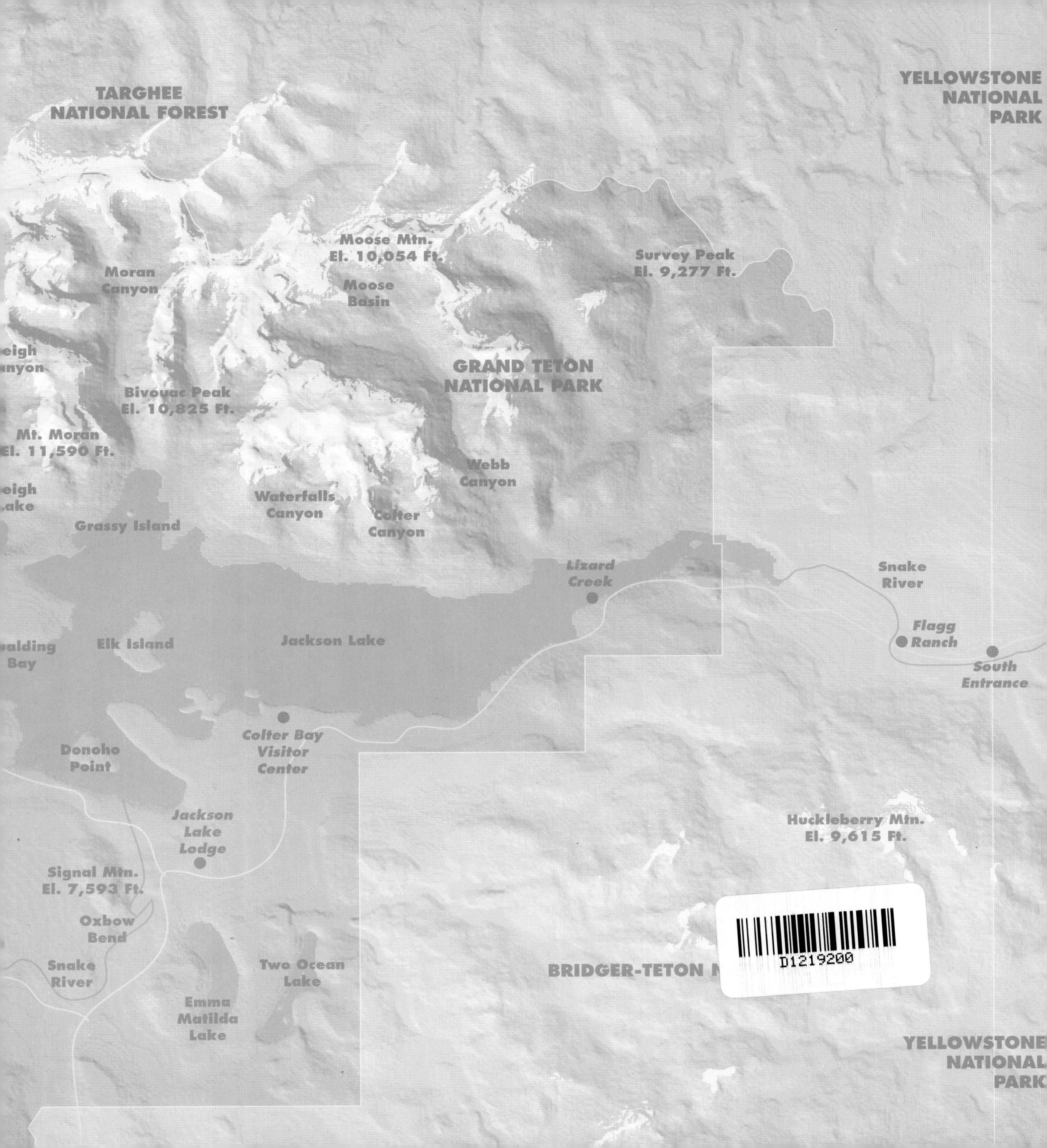

TARGHEE
NATIONAL FOREST

YELLOWSTONE
NATIONAL
PARK

Moose Mtn.
El. 10,054 Ft.

Survey Peak
El. 9,277 Ft.

Moran
Canyon

Moose
Basin

GRAND TETON
NATIONAL PARK

eigh
anyon

Bivouac Peak
El. 10,825 Ft.

Mt. Moran
El. 11,590 Ft.

Webb
Canyon

eigh
ake

Waterfalls
Canyon

Colter
Canyon

Grassy Island

Snake
River

Lizard
Creek

alding
Bay

Elk Island

Jackson Lake

Flagg
Ranch

South
Entrance

Donoho
Point

Colter Bay
Visitor
Center

Jackson
Lake
Lodge

Huckleberry Mtn.
El. 9,615 Ft.

Signal Mtn.
El. 7,593 Ft.

Oxbow
Bend

Snake
River

Two Ocean
Lake

BRIDGER-TETON N

Emma
Matilda
Lake

YELLOWSTONE
NATIONAL
PARK

"These are impossible mountains. Rock doesn't do that. Rock doesn't soar upwards with such singular dominance, such gravity-defying grace. . . . The Tetons don't merely scrape the sky, they occupy it."

JEREMY SCHMIDT

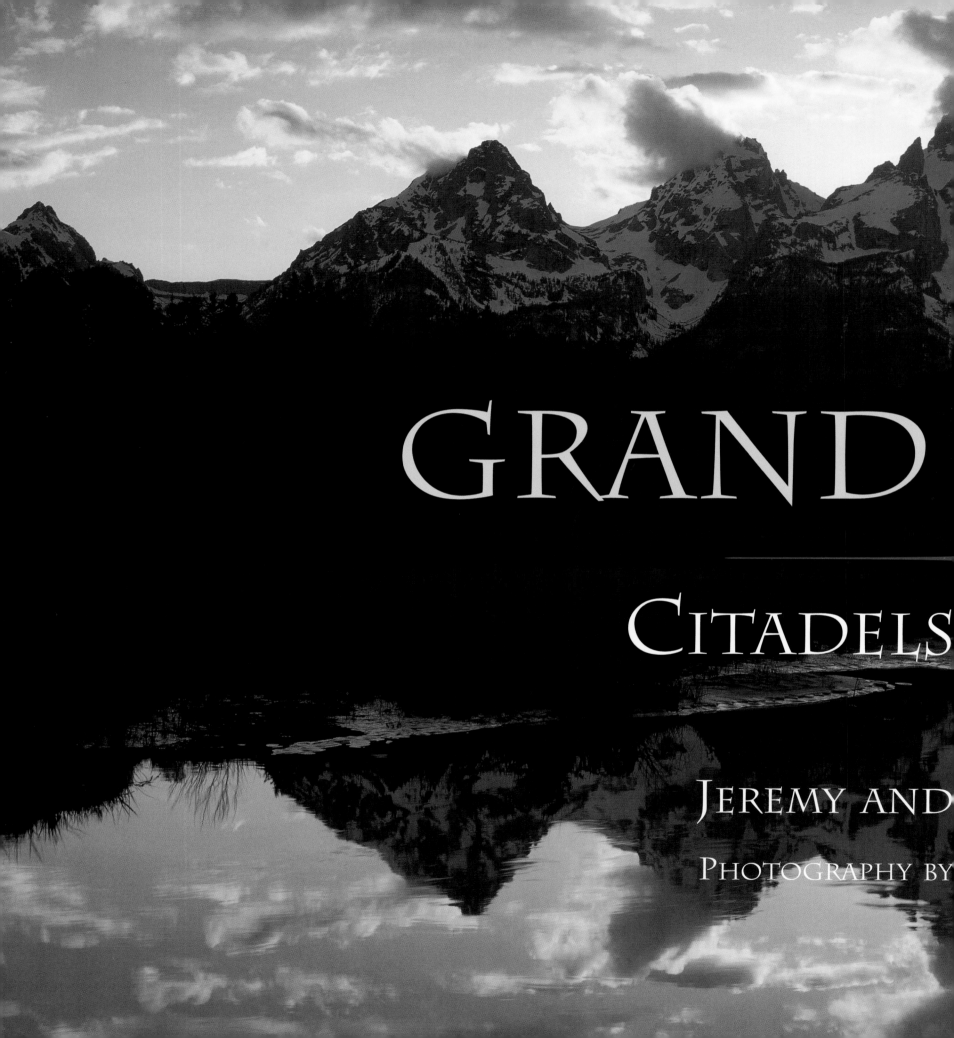

GRAND

CITADELS

JEREMY AND

PHOTOGRAPHY BY

TETON

OF STONE

THOMAS SCHMIDT

WILLARD AND KATHY CLAY

THUNDER BAY
P·R·E·S·S

A TEHABI BOOK

PAGE 1:

Acheerful cluster of arrow-leaf balsam-root grows along a buck-and-rail fence at the foot of the Teton Range.

PAGES 2-3:

Dawn breaks on a cold winter's morning, illuminating the Teton Range at Blacktail Pond Overlook.

PAGES 4-5:

The Snake River winds through a thick cotton-wood grove on its way through the valley.

PAGES 6-7:

Seen from Signal Hill, wildflowers bloom under bright blue skies.

PAGES 8-9:

The sun sets over the Teton Range and the Snake River at Schwabacher Landing.

TEHABI BOOKS

Tehabi Books conceived, designed, and produced *Grand Teton: Citadels of Stone* and has conceived and produced many award-winning books that are recognized for their strong literary and visual content. Tehabi works with national and international publishers, corporations, institutions, and nonprofit groups to identify, develop, and implement comprehensive publishing programs. The name *Tehabi* is derived from a Hopi Indian legend and symbolizes the importance of teamwork. Tehabi Books is located in San Diego, California. www.tehabi.com

President: Chris Capen
Senior Vice President: Tom Lewis
Vice President, Development: Andy Lewis
Vice President, Technology: Sam Lewis
Editorial Director: Nancy Cash
Director, Sales and Marketing: Tim Connolly
Director, Corporate Publishing and Promotions:
    Eric Pinkham
Director, Trade Relations: Marty Remmell
Series Editor: Susan Wels
Copy Editor: Jeff Campbell
Proofreader: Anne Hayes

Written by Jeremy and Thomas Schmidt, *Grand Teton: Citadels of Stone* features the photography of Willard Clay and Kathy Clay. Supplemental photography was provided by Tom and Pat Leeson (page 86) and Jeff Foott (pages 100–119). Technical, 3-D illustrations were produced by Sam Lewis. Source materials for the illustrations were provided as digital elevation models from the United States Geological Survey. Additional illustrations were produced by Andy Lewis and Tom Lewis.

Thunder Bay Press
An imprint of the Advantage Publishers Group
5880 Oberlin Drive, San Diego, CA 92121-4794
www.advantagebooksonline.com

ISBN 1-57145-786-0
Library of Congress Cataloging-in-Publication Data available upon request.

1 2 3 4 5 06 05 04 03 02

For more information on Grand Teton National Park, Thunder Bay Press and Tehabi Books encourage readers to contact the Grand Teton Natural History Association at P.O. Box 170, Moose, WY 83012; (307) 739-3406.

The paper used in this publication meets the minimum requirements of the American National Standard for Information Sciences–Permanence of Paper for Printed Library materials, ANSI z39.48-1984.

Printed in Hong Kong through Dai Nippon Printing Company.

GRAND TETON

CITADELS OF STONE

Jeremy writes: I have lived near the Tetons for over twenty years, and I feel as if they've been a part of me for a much longer time. One of my clearest childhood memories is of seeing photographs of the Tetons in a magazine and thinking, "People actually get to walk there!" It was the first time a landscape had ever spoken to me through pictures. The mountains pulled with a magnetic force. As soon as I had a drivers license and a little money in my pocket (it took very little), I headed for the Rockies every chance I got, every summer, every school holiday. When at last I was a legal adult, free from the requirements of what some people considered higher education and after the Selective Service had given up on me, I came straight here, to northwest Wyoming—what we now call the Greater Yellowstone Ecosystem, a region of relatively intact wild country comprised of two national parks, six national forests, a dozen mountain ranges, and as many designated wilderness areas. I hesitate to say that the Tetons are the heart of this magnificent, protected, and forever threatened landscape, for this is a landscape with many sacred centers, and anyway, its true heart lies somewhere in the realm of spirit. But certainly, the Tetons are a primary focal point. They continue to serve as a magnetic pole for my personal compass.

I am clearly not alone in this. My brother Thomas felt the same draw, and with his wife, Terese, made the same move. Our families live on opposite sides of the range—his on the west, mine on the east; the mountains that stand between us are more a connection than a barrier.

Mountain Men

* * *

Thomas writes: Hardly a barrier. The "treacherous Teton Pass" that so many news magazines have hyped in articles about Life in the New West must be one of the most beautiful commutes in the world. Hundreds of refugees from Jackson's pricey real estate market (a post-Jeremy boom) make the drive every day from their homes in Teton Valley, Idaho—my side of The Pass—to their jobs in Jackson. They zip past moose in the river bottoms, climb through subalpine forests, career around curves upholstered with wildflowers, and then gaze down on Jackson Hole from the bosky heights above the valley floor. The Tetons a barrier? Ha! All the world should have such barriers. Jer's right. They're a bridge. A bridge between brothers, for sure. We meet at The Pass and ski to Jer's for a wee dram. We rendezvous on my side for Grand Targhee's powder and a pint of my homebrew. We muster on the Snake amid paddles and life jackets for the whitewater, traipse the canyons and meadows for the birds and flowers, and just to scratch the wanderer's persistent itch.

But, as anyone can see, the Tetons are much more than a bridge between brothers—more than a bridge between communities, watersheds, and valleys. Touch a cliff in the central Tetons and you've forged a link with the origins of the planet. Heft a chunk of limestone imbedded with fossils and you've spanned 500 million years of evolution. Exchange a glance with an elk. Step carefully around a browsing moose. Watch a coyote jump a ground squirrel. Smell the muck of a marsh, or the dainty scent of a flower in heat. Feel the chill of evening drift down from the high canyons and sleep under the startling, gleaming smear of the Milky Way. These encounters, and many more within the Tetons, can connect us with something priceless, something real, something rare—something too-often disparaged, disdained, and dismissed in our time. They connect us with something wild—and in so doing, they bring us full circle with ourselves.

Ah-ahem, as our chum Peter Koedt would say, to bring us back to the business at hand. . . . In writing this book, Jeremy and I agreed that I would take the expository material —the third, fourth, and fifth chapters, covering the geology, plants, and animals—while he dealt with more personal aspects in the first, second, and sixth chapters. We should have known we wouldn't respect the boundaries. Jeremy has dipped into natural history, and we have both strayed into matters of the heart because the two are inseparable. You can't know the facts of this place without sensing its spirit. We hope we've communicated something of both.

A crush of wild-flowers embraces the shoreline of tiny Pass Lake—a sunny sort of place that makes you want to pull the hat over your eyes and nod off to the music of the bee-loud glade.

Before every wilderness outing, my friend Peter Koedt and I have the same—I suppose I should call it a discussion. He likes an early start, preferably before dawn. He says he enjoys watching sunrise as he whistles merrily along some misty alpine trail.

In theory, I understand and agree. Dawn is a beautiful time in the mountains. But in practice, at least for me, the appeal of sunrise is often lost in a sleepy, grumpy haze made no better by the happy chirping of a dawn zealot. Being awake and alert at 5:00 A.M. represents for me a rarely attainable goal of dubious value. "Peter," I say, "if I'm going to walk in the dark, I'd rather do it in the evening. Anyway what's special about sunrise? It's just sunset in reverse."

I take some encouragement from a friend who telephones on occasion from France. "I am sorry," he says (and he means it), "I think I have called too early." When I assure him that I really am awake at 9:30, he says, "Yes, yes, I am always forgetting. You Americans start your day so early."

This time we're getting a French start, which explains why Peter and I are setting out from the Phillips Canyon Trailhead at the civilized hour of noon. It is the first week of March. We have forty miles and four days ahead of us.

By a peculiarity of geography, the line dividing the Teton

The golden light of a winter's dawn strikes the highest ramparts of the Tetons, while the Snake River curves through a forest of cottonwood, aspen, and evergreen below the park's Snake River Overlook.

THE WINDY HEART OF WINTER

INTO THE BACKCOUNTRY

Range into its eastern and western drainages does not follow the highest peaks. Rather, it takes a gentler course through meadows and broken forest, offering a spectacular grandstand route through the heart of the range. Beginning near Teton Pass above the town of Wilson, this trail—called the Teton Crest—goes straight north along the divide, passing the central peaks on their western flanks. Although it continues all the way to Yellowstone, we plan to exit via Cascade Canyon to Jenny Lake.

By three o'clock Peter and I are sweating our way up the long incline of Phillips Canyon. Sun beats down from a clear sky. The snow throws its heat back in my face. My feet trudge mechanically. Overwarm, I stop to pull off my sweater, apply more sun-block lotion to exposed skin, and take a long drink of water.

We have waited half the winter for just these conditions. A week of unusually warm days alternating with cold nights has consolidated the snow surface. The entire range is encased in a rigid cast, meaning avalanche hazard is near zero and trailbreaking will be easy. Even better, a fast-moving storm two days ago added a dusting of soft powder, giving the surface a fresh look and the feeling of satin underfoot.

Several years ago, I came at this trail from the other end, walking down from the north. It was summer. I wandered the high meadows in a state of euphoria, feeling the sense of release that can be gotten only in the wildest and most remote places. North of Mount Moran I saw virtually no sign of hikers, not so much as a campfire scar or a boot print, but everywhere, leading in all directions, ran the stories of animals. I found grizzly tracks in places where I'd been told there were only black bears—which only reinforced the sense of wildness and made me walk with eyes and ears more widely open. There were bighorn sheep prints everywhere above timberline, and several times I saw the fleet-footed creatures themselves. I trod with guilty heart through meadows so dense in wildflowers that it was impossible not to crush hundreds.

How different it looks in winter, which is, after all, the predominant condition of the Tetons. Above nine thousand feet, summer comes and goes like a waking dream, a hallucination flickering briefly between snowfalls. In places, summer never comes at all.

From October to July, the alpine landscape becomes a snowscape—not a uniform, featureless sheet of snow, but a continually changing vista that chronicles the winter. In its shape and texture I can read where the wind has blown and where it hasn't. I can see the effects of sunshine and shade. Although it smoothes them out, the snow reflects the shapes of buried objects—fallen trees, boulders, ponds, streambeds. Beneath my skis, water tumbles over rounded rocks, the music of its passing swallowed up by eight feet or more of snow.

Warm weather causes the snow to sag and mold itself tighter to the landscape. Ripple marks, like wrinkles on the hide of an old elephant, bend around trees and boulders. I think of them as signs of age and experience: wise snow.

The last wisps of a winter storm clear over the Tetons. Most years, the passing storms maintain a base of at least four feet of snow on the floor of the valley and much more in the high country.

In the Washakie Range northeast of Jackson Hole, a strip of open water catches the reflected glow of Brooks and Sublette Mountains. Winters in the Tetons are deep, cold, and—at least for humans in Gore-Tex—exhilarating.

What goes on beneath that ever-changing surface? I can only imagine that alien twilight world where the snow meets the ground. Pocket gophers are busy burrowing at root level, shoving the dirt up into snow tunnels. Summer or winter, they exist in a darkness all their lives. As for voles and mice, some of them will pass through complete life cycles without knowing anything different. They can be born, become sexually mature, and die in a world of snow tunnels, dim light, and muffled sound. For some, life ends in the sudden attack of an invading ermine, itself as white as the snow except for the black tip of its tail.

I have on occasion found tiny emergent holes made by mice during the night. Their tracks wander crazily over the surface, as if the tiny creatures were moonstruck or suffering from a rodent form of cabin fever. What brings them out? Not food, certainly, and judging from the directionless tangle of tracks, not an impulse to go anywhere in particular. I imagine them in wild abandon, desiring just to get out of the dark and damp snow tunnels, get out and dance in the moonlight no matter what the risk. Risk there is, as proven by the occasional firm prints of an owl's wings marking the end of a track and a life.

My reverie is broken by the awareness that I am alone. Peter is far ahead, striding along with easy grace. This is characteristic. He is a builder of custom log houses, which means that he excels at doing graceful things with big unwieldy objects. He takes tree trunks, with their eccentric twists and bumps, and fits them to precise tolerances. Is this why he likes skiing with a pack? Over six feet tall, as thin as a fence post, he hangs fifty pounds from his shoulders and still manages to turn like a dancer.

Not I. I lurch along behind, feeling like one of those bottom-weighted clowns that always comes back upright when punched—except that I've gotten it backward. Instead of coming upright, I go back down. If only I could ski on my belly, as I've seen otters do.

In the best of times, skis become like wings. With good snow on rolling terrain, they move as if powered by magic. Miles glide by with almost no effort. But this—this overnight business, this expedition into the mountains stuff—is a different matter. I toil up the long incline from Phillips Canyon weighed down with all the junk a human needs to survive a night out in the alpine winter. My skis are heavy with climbing skins. My boots weigh several pounds each. In addition to items required at any time of year—sleeping bag, cookstove, food—I've got warm clothing, extra warm clothing, foam camp boots, extra food, snow shovel, snow saw, ski wax, tool kit, spare binding, and an electronic transceiver so rescuers can find my avalanche-buried body with the least inconvenience.

It's easy to feel sorry for yourself and to ponder the wrong turns you've made in life when the sweat drips down your back and soft muscles scream in outrage: "Back! Back to the sofa! Back to the fireside!" But then you come over the ridge, as I did that afternoon, to find your partner standing on God's Own Finest Campsite—a snow-covered promontory jutting out from surrounding cliffs, an eagle's eyrie overlooking a vast mountainscape. Heavy as our packs might be, we know that without them we'd have no choice but to turn around and start back. Instead, we drop them in the snow and sit on them, for this improbable but gorgeous place is home for the night. To make it sweet, all we have to do is pull out a couple chocolate bars, don warm jackets, and stare out at that magnificent country while the late afternoon light turns miles of snowfields from creamy yellow to burnished gold. Such a privilege it is to be here. I entertain thoughts of earned leisure, just rewards.

"Ah-ahem!" Peter clears his throat preparatory to an announcement I don't want to hear. "We'd better get an igloo built." Ever since we arrived, he's been eyeing the snow surface. Now he walks back and forth, probing with an aluminum snow saw, testing the layers for the right consistency. I've gotten so lazy sitting in the sun that I'm not sure I want to build anything. Now that my pack is solidly beneath me and no longer on my shoulders, I wish I'd brought a tent. Even moving slowly, I could have a tent pitched with my gear inside in ten minutes. Wouldn't that be simple?

But Peter is a builder. He enjoys creating shelter from natural materials, and what could be more natural and renewable than snow? He also prefers the solidity of a structure. Although I know it will take us more than an hour, I set about helping him however I can, which isn't much. He knows how to cut the blocks, how to angle them just right to create a rising spiral into which the last block drops like a keystone. Although made of water, an igloo is strong enough that you can climb up and sit on the top. I'll think about that the next time I climb the winding steps to the summit of St. Peter's Basilica.

As we work, the sun sets, and a gusty evening wind scatters the warmth of afternoon somewhere into tomorrow. Venus is already bright in the western sky as we finish the job of smoothing the frozen floor and arranging our foam pads. While I stick our skis firmly in the snow so storm winds cannot carry them away, Peter lights candles and the cookstove. The igloo glows with jack-o-lantern warmth. One of the most surprising things about an igloo is how well its frozen walls insulate. By the time I climb in, pulling the snow-door closed behind me, the domed room is already heated to around forty-five degrees from nothing more than candles, stove, and body warmth. There is room to sit up. We take off our jackets. We lie back on soft sleeping bags and pass a bourbon flask while supper bubbles fragrantly in the pot.

Let the wind blow. Let the temperature plunge. No tent was ever so comfortable. Water for drinking and cooking comes from snow that we carve out of the walls. If something spills, it soaks harmlessly into the snow floor. Going out after supper, I shiver beneath the black dome of infinite space. The spired ramparts of Rendezvous Peak groan in the wind that seems to tear down from the stars. I feel utterly exposed. The outside temperature has fallen to near ten degrees. Dressed as I am, without the igloo to crawl back into, I wouldn't last fifteen minutes.

Next morning we say goodbye to the igloo, drop down a steep powder slope, and traverse through open forest over a low pass into the head of the Middle Fork of Granite

The jagged silhouette of the Teton Range cuts across a winter sunset above Spread Creek. Snowcover, never a blank screen, subtly reflects the underlying landscape and records weather fluctuations—lashing winds, sun-baked days, sleet storms, and powder dumps.

FOLLOWING PAGES:

High above treeline, storm clouds envelop the Tetons. This is a familiar sight to many a cheerful group of backcountry skiers who have set out on a perfectly clear spring morning only to be ambushed by an afternoon stealth storm sweeping in from the West.

EVERGREEN ISLANDS

Here and there on the valley floor, islands of dense evergreen trees rise abruptly from the sparse sagebrush flats. The sudden change in vegetation is due mainly to underlying soil conditions. The trees grow on portions of moraines deposited by Ice Age glaciers, while the sagebrush grows over a sheet of gravelly debris washed out from under the glaciers. The fertile morainal soil contains silt and clay, which retain much more water than the porous quartzite gravels of the outwash plain.

Creek. Like most Teton drainages, the creek cuts a deep canyon downstream, but up here it's all rolling meadows, groves of alpine fir, sensuously rippling snow drifts.

Paying close attention to critters and their signs, I am rewarded by weasel, marten, coyote, pine squirrel, and rabbit tracks. From treetops, Clark's nutcrackers squawk like some exuberant people do when they think that no one can hear them. In winter the tracks come in pairs, the hunter and the hunted. Mouse trails on the surface end in a flurry of wing prints. Coyote tracks follow those of snowshoe hares. Marten tracks run from one grove to the next on the same routes used by pine squirrels.

Past Marion Lake, up over a bare ridge to a plateau, and we stand riveted. For there rise the central Teton peaks. It is a quality of the world's most beautiful mountains that every angle is spectacular. This is true of Everest, K2, the Matterhorn, Kilimanjaro, Fuji, Rainier, and the Grand Teton. Although most frequently pictured from the east, the Grand has no best side. It dominates all approaches. From where we stand, the South Teton, Middle Teton, and various other summits appear stacked up against its flanks. Rather than block the view, they make it all the more impressive.

But now we hurry. The wind has gained strength, whipping loose snow into a ground blizzard that stings our eyes and exposed skin. The high cloud cover, building these last few hours, thickens and drops. Soon the Grand is wreathed in banners of mist. Minutes later, it vanishes entirely, and we arrive at Fox Creek Pass in a near white-out. Rarely have I seen a storm close so fast. It comes in like a classic warm front, beginning with high thin wisps, thickening to a solid cloud cover, lowering as it advances.

Stung by the wind, we work extra fast on the igloo and climb in while daylight still remains. Feeling both snug and smug, we sit on soft foam pads in our house made of water, lit by candles, sipping bourbon, and eating hot bean stew. So well insulated from wind and sound is the igloo that our only indication of stormy weather is the occasional miniavalanche of snow that slides down the vent in the apex of the roof.

Once, in the middle of the night, snow from the vent falls on my face. I wake up enough to wonder if this is a warning.

Morning comes wrapped in cotton. We wake to a dim white glow and the long rumbling sound of a distant avalanche. Digging our way outside through a deep fresh drift, we emerge into wind-frenzied whiteness and peer toward the cliffs of the Death Canyon Shelf. Half a mile distant, the dark rocks appear and disappear in passing gusts. Cascades of snow pour off the heights only to be caught by the gale and whipped back into the air.

What to do? The next few miles are relatively safe. We could button up like space men. But there is already close to a foot of new snow, and if it keeps up, progress might get difficult. The storm has the feel of a lasting one—two or three days, perhaps. If we avoid avalanches, and make the necessary miles, we can finish the trip as planned. But we would see nothing of the mountains, and the point of this excursion is not mere exercise, nor a desire to prove we can do it.

We discuss this over breakfast.

Agreeing that discretion is the better part of enjoyment, and maybe survival, we bail out. Packed up, zipped up, everything tied tight, avalanche transceivers checked, we push off down the slope into Death Canyon. All day the snow keeps sheeting down. When we can see the canyon walls, they appear besieged; waves of snow beat against them like ocean surf. Then the clouds again draw closed, and we ski blind beneath the occasional thunder of big slides up high. Heavy gusts of wind wrack even the deep timber, and we are grateful for the relative shelter of big trees.

Actually, it is beautiful and invigorating. I feel privileged to be here. With its standard equipment, the human body is woefully inadequate to cope with winter conditions of any kind, yet here we are, warm and reasonably comfortable, thanks to good skis, parkas, goggles, packaged food, and synthetic fabrics, all produced in an industrial world that seems the complete reverse of this wild place. We are also privileged to be here now, at this time in history. Who can say how long our parks will last? In our ongoing war against nature, beauty and wildness are the first casualties; here we walk in their full, magnificent fury.

Lower, the forest grows dense, forcing us into the bed of the creek. An uneven mass of snow covers the creek, forming pillows and mushroom shapes that slow our progress. I can't hear the water below, but several times I catch a glimpse of it sliding clear and shallow over the gravel, then disappearing from sight, and I think about the trout that live year round beneath the drifts, finning in the blue, snow-roofed shadows, waiting for summer with the inscrutable patience of their kind.

I think about them three hours later with the light failing and my own patience wearing thin. What was snow at high altitude has become sleet and rain in the valley bottom. We struggle out to the road soaking wet, with three or four inches of snow stuck to the bottoms of our skis, and no amount of scraping makes it better. The skis weigh ten or fifteen pounds each, and we would walk except that the snow is armpit deep and there is no choice but to trudge on like a couple of Frankenstein's monsters. Late in the evening, we are pounding on the door of a ranch house, and it is a testimony to the enduring hospitality of Wyoming country people that the folks who live there take us in, feed us supper, and congratulate us for being smart enough to come down in such weather as this.

* * *

Three months later, we are back on the crest, trying again. After being blown out of the mountains in March, we made plans to return and complete the trip. For three months we kept our packs loaded, intending to take advantage of the first clear spell that came along. Yet the weeks wore on, through one of the wettest spring seasons on record. Our first

Crumbling ramparts of Pinnacle Ridge catch the warm glow of sunset.

clear opportunity has come in the first week of June.

How different things are now, and how much the same. It still looks like winter on Death Canyon Shelf; if anything, the snow is deeper than it was in March. But it doesn't feel like winter. The sun, wielding its full summer power, shines through a cloudless sky. In the warmth of June, we have dispensed with igloos, choosing instead to carry a light tent. Peter is wearing shorts and a T-shirt and a natty golf cap. Looking out toward the valley, we see a sweep of bright summer green. Ahead of us, drawing us on, rise the central Teton peaks.

Although the snow is wet and a bit sticky, the skiing is easy. We cruise the shelf, cross into Alaska Basin, and climb out the other side. Our route is dictated to some extent by the need to avoid falling snow: in the warm weather, enormous cornices that have gathered on the high cliffs are breaking loose and falling with thunderous explosions. Chunks the size of pickup trucks come leaping down the slopes, and the thought of being hit by one keeps us well away from the rock faces.

Winter has lost its grip. There is no bare ground in these high basins, but I can hear the tumble of meltwater beneath the snowpack, and we continually encounter the signs of animals out and about. Two coyotes work their way across an avalanche track. Juncos move through the alpine fir groves in waves, singing like warblers, and robins hop on the snow collecting the surprising variety of insect life that finds reason to be there. Marmots, having awoken and dug their way up to the surface, stand watchfully beside dirt-stained tunnels. I wonder if it's the pursuit of marmot that explains the mountain lion tracks we find nearby.

On our second night, we camp on the heights near the divide. The basin is filled with snow. The west face of the Grand towers above us. The air is warm enough that we sit out on the snow until the last reddish glow lifts from the summit of the Grand, leaving behind a world bled of color. During the night, the snow sets up as hard as an ice rink, so that when we push off from camp we sail down the canyon. Over buried timber, rough-edged talus, hummocky meadows, and streams still imprisoned by the snow, we drift light-footed like seeds of salsify.

Winter in the Tetons always seems to go out with a struggle. It spits and howls and snows way past the time anyone thinks is reasonable. But in the end it slips away quietly, as if waiting until no one is looking, and the next thing you know the flowers are blooming, and birds are singing, and the water that was snow makes music in the creekbeds. That's how it is for us on this sunny day in June—an effortless transition. The snow runs out, we take off our skis, change our boots for light running shoes, and a few minutes later are walking through wildflowers into the first bloom of summer.

Hoarfrost flocks a grove of trees beneath the Tetons. On mornings such as this—bitter cold and absolutely still—nothing seems astir in the chill woods.

Late November, early morning. I am following a coyote trail through a foot of fresh snow. The temperature is well below zero, and the snow, almost weightless, kicks up feathery in front of my boots. I started walking this morning just as the moonless dark gave way to a pale shiver of gray light in the east. Yesterday there was storm and wind over the mountains—not the first snowfall of the season but the first true winter storm, an event marked by low temperatures and ground hard-frozen, ready to accept the mantle of winter. Autumn snow is transient; it always melts off. But this stuff is here to stay.

Late last night the weather cleared, and the temperature plunged into the minus twenties. Partly to celebrate the turn of season, but also because I love moving through snow before it gets deep enough to require skis, I decided to make a dawn sortie into the foothills on the east side of Jackson Hole. Animal tracks would be fresh, and it seemed like a good idea to walk an open ridge and see what was around.

It is a busy place. Besides the track of this coyote, I find the snow churned up by dozens of elk who came through some time in the night, headed across the valley, migrating south toward the National Elk Refuge where they will spend the winter.

Mount Moran, elevation 12,605 feet, stands roughly six thousand feet above the semi-arid floor of Jackson Hole and dominates all views of the Tetons from the northern half of the park.

PEAKS OF GRANITE, PLAINS OF SAGE

LAND OF THE TETONS

This is their season of danger—they move at night to avoid hunters. Or rather, most of them do. I am part way up the sage-covered ridge when I see a group of elk break from the forest above me. They move fast, in a tight group following an old lead cow. Twenty-five, maybe thirty of them, stream out of the trees and down the open ridge toward the river bottom. Stragglers, I suppose, running late, either brave or dumb. Their breaths hang in the air like little explosions. I can hear their breathing and the muffled thunder of their hooves, mingled with the querulous mewing calls that cows and calves use to keep track of one another.

They have cleared the forest by several hundred yards before the bulls emerge, five of them striding tentatively at first, then breaking into a dead run, heads lowered, antlers held back. Hunting season has just ended, but they don't know that yet. They move like animals in a guerrilla war, drawn forward by the need to migrate along their ancient paths but fully aware of the danger of open country. Ahead of them, spurred on by them, the cows and calves also break into a run. Down to the river, across the willow flats, over a low hill, they gallop for several miles before I lose sight of them. They will be the last to come through until tonight, when darkness gives the next wave of migrants courage to move.

From here, following my coyote track becomes a challenge. The elk have thoroughly ruined the neat line of his footprints. But I know where he was headed. There is no sense for man or coyote to do anything here but go up.

As I near the top of the ridge, the sun breaks free from the eastern horizon, bathing me in orange light and making it marginally easier to distinguish coyote sign among the chaos of elk tracks. I read his story as well as I can: here he turns toward the forest, sniffing among the trunks of big fir trees, digging in the soft duff around a pine squirrel midden. Here he marks a stone with a squirt of yellow; a bit farther, he adds his comment to the metal disk of a geodetic survey marker. Walking on, I ponder the overlapping dominions of *Homo sapiens* and *Canis latrans* and suddenly realize that there are now two sets of prints. No, three. My coyote has been joined by two others.

It is a natural human response, I suppose, to become so engrossed in details as to forget one's surroundings. My mind's eye is fully occupied with picturing three coyotes dancing around each other as if playing. They run circles through the trees, dash out onto the sage-covered ridge and back into the forest. I follow, keeping my nose to the ground and my thoughts in the immediate past, as the sun rises higher into the sky. I have topped the ridge; I have moved some distance before some impulse finally penetrates my concentration and causes me to look up. Immediately all thoughts of coyotes vanish.

Ten miles away, across a sea of cloud that fills the valley, the Tetons rocket upward through the mist. White with new snow, they shine in early morning light, and the view startles me. I knew they were there, of course, but now I stand frozen as if seeing them for the first time. I have lived near these mountains for over twenty years. From one angle or

Pinnacle Ridge, one of the most prominent mountains in the Washakie Range, rises above the snow-packed meadows of Togwotee (TOE-guh-dee) Pass. The Washakies wall off the northeastern end of Jackson Hole.

TOPOGRAPHY OF
THE TETONS

As if to demonstrate once and for all the difference between mountains and flat land, the Tetons rise abruptly from the sage-covered floor of Jackson Hole. Most ranges are bulwarked by foothills, their approaches guarded by outlying ramparts. Not so these archetypal peaks riding their faulted block upward while the valley floor sinks at their feet.

The Grand Teton (13,770 feet), the Middle Teton (12,804), the South Teton (12,514), Mount Owen (12,928), and Teewinot (12,325) occupy the center of the range, and are bracketed by two impressive canyons named Death and Cascade. Mount Moran (12,605) stands separate to the north, a graceful peak marked by two distinctive glaciers and a summit that only looks flat; it is actually a narrow ridge dropping steeply to the east and west.

So many aspects of the landscape collide in opposites: horizontal and vertical, craggy and rounded. The Tetons' eastern wall is steep, its western slope is gradual. Valleys on both sides—Jackson Hole and Teton Valley—are frying-pan flat.

The sagebrush flats of Jackson Hole are hemmed in by mountains rising all around. There are the Tetons, of course, to the west. To the north lie the billowing, lumpish contours of Yellowstone's lava flows; to the northeast, the Washakie Range. The gentle terrain of the Mount Leidy Highlands and the Gros Ventre Range wall off the valley's east and southeast margins. Then, closing off the valley to the south and southwest come the Hoback and Snake River ranges.

Snake River   Blacktail Butte   Grand Teton National   Granite Canyon   Open Canyon   Death Canyon   Death Canyon
                                              Park Boundry   Phelps Lake   Shelf

On both sides of the Tetons, water tumbles down from snowfields and glaciers, pouring through canyons carved during the ice ages. Streams on the west side collect in Teton River, which flows north through Teton Valley before bending around the Big Hole Mountains and joining the Henry's Fork River, a tributary of the Snake River.

Meanwhile, streams on the east side of the Tetons gather their waters in a gem-like string of lakes whose basins themselves were carved by Pleistocene glaciers: Jackson Lake, Leigh Lake, String, Jenny, Taggart, Bradley, and Phelps— all of them hard beneath vaulting cliffs. The largest of these lakes, Jackson Lake, is made still bigger by a dam that raises its waters thirty-seven feet above their natural level. It is fed primarily by the Snake River, which flows out of Yellowstone National Park. Seeking a path toward the Pacific Ocean, the

Snake finds a weakness in the mountain barrier at the south end of Jackson Hole, punches through an impressive gorge in a rollick of whitewater, and rushes west to pick up the Henry's Fork before heading across the deserts of southern Idaho.

Crossing the range is difficult, usually joyous, work. Highway 22 crests the divide at Teton Pass, climbing 10 percent grades and testing radiators and brakes. Highway 89 follows the river through its tortuous canyon. The only other crossing is a rough dirt road that bumps along

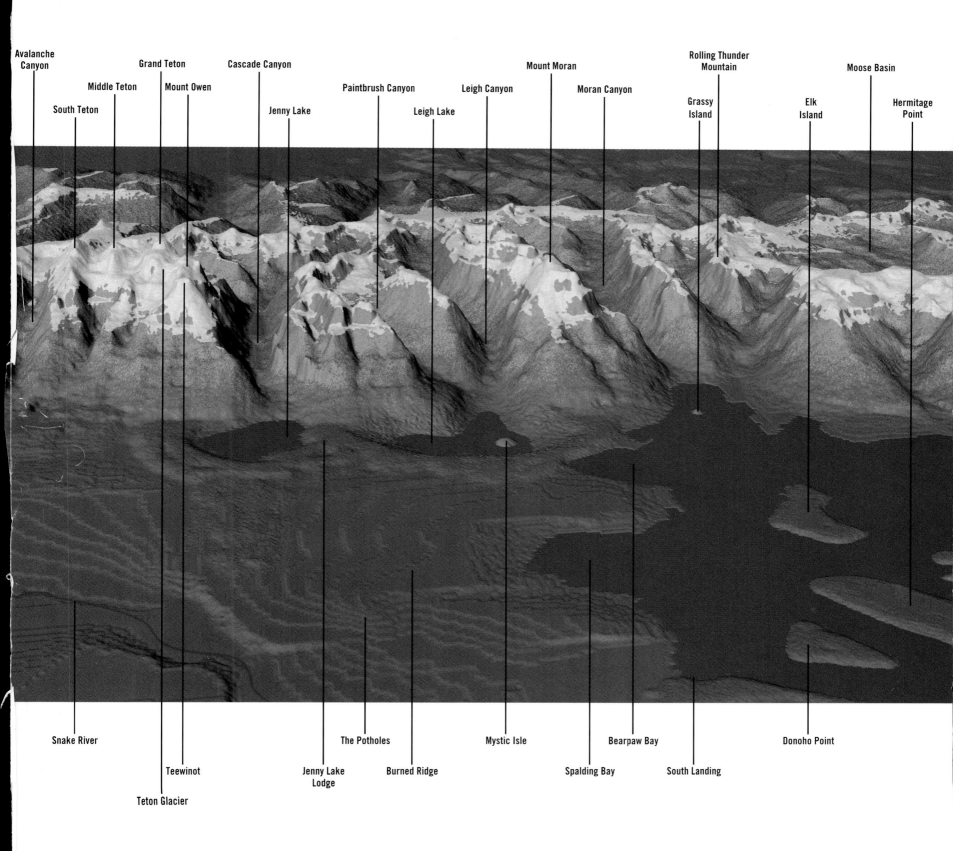

Avalanche Canyon

Grand Teton

Cascade Canyon

Rolling Thunder Mountain

Middle Teton

Mount Owen

Mount Moran

Moose Basin

Paintbrush Canyon

Leigh Canyon

Moran Canyon

South Teton

Jenny Lake

Leigh Lake

Grassy Island

Elk Island

Hermitage Point

Snake River

The Potholes

Mystic Isle

Bearpaw Bay

Donoho Point

Teewinot

Jenny Lake Lodge

Burned Ridge

Spalding Bay

South Landing

Teton Glacier

another, I see them almost every day unless stormy weather obscures them, and even then they are never far from my mind.

None of that matters. It makes no difference how familiar to me these mountains are. In every fresh glimpse lies an element of surprise, a deep-seated omigawd reaction that no amount of experience can diminish. The synapses refuse to learn. They always fire a new warning, as if to say this is wrong, these are impossible mountains. Rock doesn't do that. Rock doesn't soar upwards with such singular dominance, such gravity-defying grace. At least never in nature. Like opera scenery pushed up from below the stage in a puff of theatrical smoke, the Tetons look almost but not quite real. A stage designer's idea of mountains: no foothills to occlude their upward thrust, no rival peaks in sight. The Tetons don't merely scrape the sky, they occupy it.

Like opera scenery, the Tetons look almost two-dimensional, a sheer wall of rock—not much up there but snow, ice, and trees hanging on by their toenails. Surely anything that comes loose up there among the slippery crags must come down, all the way down, landing on the valley floor, splat, like pigeon droppings at the base of the Empire State Building.

In a geologic sense this is true. Everything up there is on its way down. But like all things worth knowing, the Tetons possess hidden complexity—valleys, meadows, alpine lakes, meandering creeks, expanses of rolling alpine tundra. A quick scan of the map shows the high country dotted with lakes. I count dozens. I've camped beside a number of them, and they always seem a bit contradictory. In a primarily vertical landscape, lakes are as unexpected and precious as springs in the desert. They are oases of calm where meltwater pauses to regain its composure before continuing its wild plunge to the valley bottom.

Before going further, we need to clear up some nomenclature. The mountains were named for the three most prominent peaks seen from the west side—the Grand Teton, the Middle Teton, and the South Teton—that anchor a mountain range also called the Tetons. While the Tetons are indisputably grand, there is only one Grand Teton, which at 13,770 feet high is the central spire of the range. The mountains stretch for about forty miles, emerging from the volcanic flows of Yellowstone on their north end and blending gracefully with lesser ranges at their southern extremity. The Tetons are a narrow range, practically a single line of peaks with a steep eastern face and a more gentle western slope. While the structure is in fact a bit more complicated than that, the image is useful for an overview.

The western slope drains into the Teton River and the Henry's Fork of the Snake River. The dominant stream for the region is the main stem of the Snake River, which rises in the Teton Wilderness just outside Yellowstone National Park's southeast boundary. The Snake winds through Yellowstone for some distance, then turns south and makes a gravelly run past the Tetons, picking up strength and other rivers as it goes. About twenty miles south of Grand Teton National Park, it turns west, punches a canyon through the mountains, picks up

A *wild, glorious season, winter is welcomed at the outset as a returning hero—toasted, feted, celebrated throughout the lengthening evenings. But it holds forth long after its hosts have stopped slapping it on the back and have begun to stifle yawns. Not until the planet tilts insistently toward the sun does it finally stagger from the region in a howling, raging fit, spitting sleet and hail and sometimes burying the place in the year's deepest snowfall.*

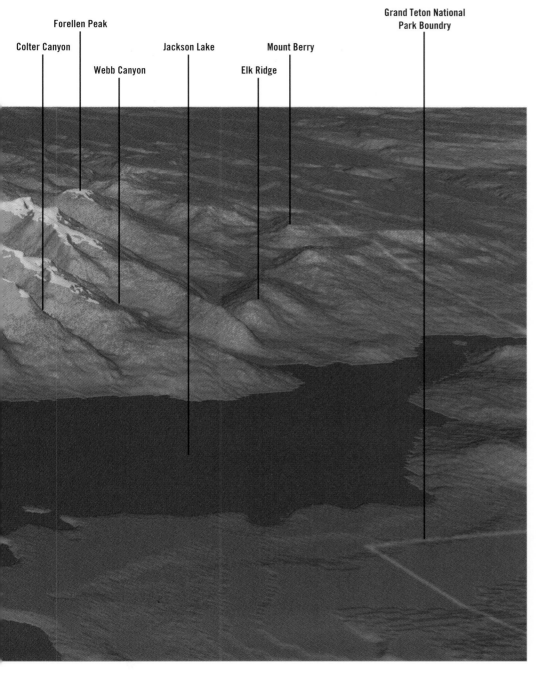

Colter Canyon

Forellen Peak

Webb Canyon

Jackson Lake

Elk Ridge

Mount Berry

Grand Teton National
Park Boundry

the interglacial periods of the great Ice Age—so recent that man himself could almost remember. . . . It is exhilarating to think that the surge of life on our planet is older than the earth features we now can see."

NOTE: Although it may look like a photograph, this image is actually a computerized, extruded, topographic view. It was created using digital elevation models derived from the United States Geological Survey (USGS) satellite maps and traditional, flat USGS topographic maps.

To prepare the extruded topo map, data from the USGS was downloaded from the Earth Science Information Center to a personal computer and converted into a three-dimensional model. There, a flat or "birds-eye" version was rendered which simulates a direct overhead view of the region (the end sheets on both inside covers of this book were reproduced from this version). The flat version was then tilted in order to create a view of the area from an angle eighteen degrees off the horizon. Shadows, textures, and colors were added to represent a view that one might see from space.

the edge of the Yellowstone plateau between the two national parks. These routes have been used by human travelers and migrating animals since far before there were cars and motorhomes to overheat on warm summer days.

It is easy to feel small and fragile when looking at these old and powerful mountains. But naturalist Olaus Murie, in his book *Wapiti Wilderness*, considers the possibility that the Teton landscape you see today may be relatively young. "Perhaps the mountain sculpture we see here today was largely accomplished in one of

The Tetons, black
against the setting sun,
jut roughly six thousand
feet above Jackson
Lake.

the Henry's Fork, and heads purposefully across the arid, volcanic plains of Idaho.

Back in fur trade days, mountain men used the word "hole" to describe a valley ringed by mountains. Up in Montana, for example, there is the Bighole. In Yellowstone, there is the Firehole. On the west side of the Tetons is Pierre's Hole, while on their east side— named, it is said, for Davy Jackson, a fur trapper who spent a lot of time here in the 1820s—lies Jackson Hole. Originally (and still by some old-timers), it was called Jackson's Hole, until some official with an aversion to apostrophes chopped off its tail. There is also Jackson Lake, a once-natural alpine lake enlarged and used for irrigation water storage since 1907, when the Jackson Lake Dam was built. Jackson, the community, is a growing—many would say exploding—town on the southern edge of the national park.

In this quick survey we should also take note of the Gros Ventre Mountains— the Grow-vahnts—which rise with gentler, more conventional manners on the east side of Jackson Hole. Their rolling, bemeadowed slopes provide a pleasing balance to the radical posture of the Tetons. By eighteenth-century European aesthetics, the Gros Ventres would be a suitable picnicking area, a landscape of meadows and polite deciduous trees. On a quiet summer day you can almost imagine coach-and-fours rolling through the parklike surroundings while wigged and powdered gentlefolk make snooty conversation and flash lace kerchiefs. A place not too primitive to take the ladies for a day among the wildflowers. But! Protect their eyes from the scene across the valley! For there stand the Tetons, with their dark dripping forest and frowning crags. Terrible, frightening, uncouth in all aspects—including their lascivious French name.

Of course, the only people here in the eighteenth century were Native Americans—Shoshoni, Crow, Nez Perce, and others, who along with their predecessors had been traveling through the Tetons for thousands of years. It was they who established travel routes that are still in use today, including Teton Pass and the Gros Ventre River valley. They made tools and points from the obsidian in several local quarries and carved bowls from native steatite, a soft rock found on the Tetons' western slope. Although they left no written impressions, it seems impossible that they did not regard this landscape as special. It has been generally thought that they moved through in the summer, but recent evidence points toward winter habitation, which comes as no surprise to those who have learned to love the cold season in Jackson Hole.

With a few exceptions like Osborne Russell, mountain men of the fur trapping period rarely wrote about their feelings, but they lived like aristocracy of a different kind, lording it over a land regulated only by natural laws, their lives governed primarily by personal courage and ability. You wonder what Jim Bridger, who called Pierre's Hole the most perfect mountain valley in the Rockies, would think about property values today. He might recall how he roamed free across what are now million-dollar acres, never encountering a security-gated

In a sense, spring lasts all summer in the Tetons. It starts on the floor of Jackson Hole, then follows the receding snowline up the flanks of the mountains. If you miss spring on the valley floor, you can probably catch up with it somewhere in the high country.

community or a "Keep Out" sign, and I suspect he'd say he was there during the richest time.

In 1892 Owen Wister wrote, "Of all places in the Rocky Mountains that I know, it is the most beautiful, and, as it lies too high for man to build and prosper, its trees and waters should be kept from man's irresponsible destruction." Although his sentiments toward preservation were ahead of their time, he was clearly wrong on the prosperity issue. Wister had no way of foretelling what an industry could be made from snow and scenery. More than that, I suspect he had an exaggerated view of a Teton winter. True, it does get mighty cold in Jackson Hole—below minus sixty on a few memorable occasions. But it's colder in Minnesota for much of the winter, thanks to subzero air masses that move into the upper Midwest and stay for weeks at a time. That doesn't happen in the Rockies. Nor do other parts of the country enjoy the warming benefits of high-altitude sunshine. This is something many westerners would just as soon keep secret: the surprisingly mild, sunny days of February.

They forget March. Forgetting March is a survival mechanism.

There's an old saying about spring in the Rockies—it lasts about two days between winter and summer, and then summer lasts only a week. The rest of the year is winter. But this is wrong. Spring is a distinct and long-lived season. It begins on a warm day in March while even the valley floor remains locked firmly in ice. It arrives in the company of a south wind streaming over the snowbound hills carrying with it the smell of ground thawing somewhere out in Idaho. It's not much more than a whiff of sagebrush and mud, but to noses accustomed to the spare odors of winter, it seems loaded with exotic perfume. Thoughts turn toward tropical beaches, burning desert sands, bare feet on warm grass.

A cruel hunger: There will be snow in April. There will be snow in May, too, carried along on some of the year's most unpredictable, or—as the forecasters like to say—unsettled, weather. It's not clear if this refers to the natural climate or the human one. May is historically the wettest month of the Teton year, with June a close second. The moisture comes as sleet, snow, rain, and tears. Whoever can do it gets out of the valley, heads for warmer climes. Those who remain behind kick the mud, fondle their seed catalogs, and vibrate with impatience. In some years, consistently warm weather (which means seventy degrees in these parts) doesn't roll in until late June. As much as they might love winter, spring is the season that tries men's and women's souls.

I try to see it from the wild creatures' perspective. In early May, while snow lies soggy in three-foot slushpiles beneath dripping conifers and the sky spits gray drizzle, I hear the ecstatic whiffle of a snipe rising and falling over the marshlands. From high overhead, so high that even such large birds are pinpoints in the sky, comes the unmistakable clattering ululation of sandhill cranes circling, circling. Out along the river, the eggs of Canada geese are already hatching, and moose that spent the heart of winter deep in the conifers show up among shrub willows along river bottoms.

H*igh summer in the Tetons, and still the frigid waters of Jackson Lake deter all but the hardiest swimmers. Rounded cobbles such as these along the shore of Little Mackinaw Bay also line the bed of the Snake River.*

Then one day out on the National Elk Refuge, an old cow elk turns her head toward Mount Leidy and starts walking. By deep wisdom, or some biological signal, she knows that the time is right. Others take her lead. Strung out single file in groups of a dozen or a hundred, thousands of animals begin moving north, and for a time the plains near the town of Kelly resemble Africa's Serengeti. The bulls, having dropped their old antlers, already sport velvet-covered knobs of new ones. I imagine they feel light-headed and frisky. In contrast, the cows carry increasingly weighty burdens; their calves will be born in June, on ancestral calving grounds.

And still summer hangs tantalizing in the wings, but rarely does it stay away past its official, astronomical beginning on June twenty-first. By then the valley is in full bloom and the high mountain trails are generally free of snow.

Is it the shortness of the season that gives summer such a poignant beauty? It lasts only a few glorious weeks, and all living things respond. Life explodes in a sweet jubilation of growth, giving an illusion of lushness that belies the rest of the year. Summer is nature on a spending spree. By mid-August, high meadows will already be showing signs of autumn, drying up, turning brown, and crackling in the breeze.

For all the wild partying of summer, the blossoms and perfumes and soft air, I think of autumn as the most beautiful season. The animals are fat. Their young, those that have survived, are strong. Flowers will die, but their seeds have been scattered. Animals face the uncertainty of winter, but their seeds, too, have been sown. By the arrival of the first permanent snow, the next generations of deer, elk, moose, bison, and many other creatures are securely planted in mothers' wombs, the fires of life banked for the next growing season.

The death of summer brings on the brief glory of autumn. The death of winter makes room for spring. Yet even in death itself there is beauty—not just in its promise of rebirth, and its reiteration of the profound cycle of life and the year's seasons, but in the artifacts of life, the dead things themselves. In civilized and cultivated landscapes, dead things aren't allowed to linger on the landscape. The grass is cut, the crops harvested, the deadfall cleaned up. Not so in the Tetons, where the bleached skull of an elk can lie undisturbed, growing lichen on its shady side while plants reach up through its various cavities and take it back to the soil. There is beauty in the scattered, white-shining bones of a field mouse, in the delicacy of frosted vegetation, in the way marsh grass curls when it dries, and in the weathered appearance of a cottonwood snag. I have stood in old burns where the wind blew through hollowed knotholes of dead trees—the wind playing them like flutes, making wilderness music. No one has cut them down, no one has cleaned up the so-called mess, no one has made them into something to sell and call useful. Blessed are the useless, for they enrich the margins of our lives.

Autumn, perhaps the most beautiful and certainly the most bittersweet season in the Tetons, touches a field of yarrow and grass near Oxbow Bend.

A*spens blaze against a cloud bank. Autumn strips the leaves and causes grass and wildflowers to wither and rot. Weak animals may die, and yet not all is death. The seeds of next year's lives have already been planted.*

It's mid-July, high summer in the Teton Range, and my arm flops lazily from the car window as I drive into the forest at the base of Signal Mountain. By now the warmth of the season has turned aside all thoughts of winter and snow—even of the endless dreary spring with its persistent frigid damp, its wind-driven sleet, rain, mud, and confinement. Today, the welcome heat calls for shorts and sandals, for leisurely strolls, for indolence, sloth, and perhaps, for contemplation. Thus Signal Mountain. No summit in the park requires so little in the way of mountaineering skills (a steady foot on the gas pedal does it). Yet this unpretentious hump of forested rock offers perhaps the finest overall view of the Tetons, the surrounding terrain, and the underlying geologic story.

I do my best to pay attention to the narrow road, but the day is too sweet and the warm breeze too rich with the dreamy scent of resin for prudent driving. My eyes keep drifting to the passing, slender columns of lodgepole pine and especially to the open, grassy floor beneath them. The understory is radiant, dappled with shifting pools of yellow-green light, cool emerald shadows, and now and then, startling flashes of crimson. It takes a moment for the identification to sink in, because I rarely see the flower in such a vivid shade of red, but it's Indian paintbrush, all right.

The hollow thump of a tire edging off the pavement

The Grand Teton, highest of Wyoming's youngest mountains, catches the first rays of light above Cascade Canyon's North Fork.

HEAVED AGAINST THE SKY

BIRTH OF THE MOUNTAINS

Lush alpine meadows stretch beneath the sedimentary cliffs of Fossil Mountain near Fox Pass in the Jedediah Wilderness Area.

and the gleam of oncoming chrome snaps me back to the business of driving. Soon, I reach Jackson Point Overlook, with its grandstand view of the abrupt and imposing wall of the Tetons. At first, all that registers is that jaw-dropping row of peaks—mile upon mile of pinnacles, crags, and great hulking domes of gray rock jutting six thousand to seven thousand feet above the valley floor and cutting across the entire western skyline. Then the eye strays downward to the broad but irregular outline of Jackson Lake, with its islands and bays, coves, and long fingers of land stretching along the base of the Teton Range. Dark masses of evergreen forest border the lake, reaching off to the left and out onto the vast, olive-green surface of the valley. My eyes follow the mountains into the distant south, where the rumpled foothills of lesser ranges close the valley.

With mountains rising on all sides of this magnificent, oblong crater of a valley, it's easy to see why the fur trappers called it a "hole." But before it became a hole, it was part of a broad uplift of highlands. And before that, part of a sea floor. And before that, well, about the best one can say is that parts of it lay miles and miles beneath the earth's surface where intense heat and pressure warped, bent, folded, swirled, and utterly changed the rocks from whatever they had been into what they would become nearly 3 billion years later—the core of the Teton Range.

There's a lot to see from the sunny overlook on Signal Mountain. Hawks comb the thermals. Butterflies twirl over the wildflowers. Chipmunks scoot through the brush and nose out onto the asphalt path to find lunch. But the eye tends to linger on the ragged pyramid of the Grand Teton, the flattish summit of Mount Moran, and the whole, glorious mass of fractured naked rock between them. Heaved upward, deeply eroded, and carved apart by enormous glaciers, that wall of peaks vividly exposes the ancient core of the range.

Simply put, the core is a mish-mash of fine-grained, salt-and-pepper granite pushed into a marble-cake swirl of metamorphic rock. Walk up any canyon in the central Tetons and you'll see these swirling, black and white bands of gneiss and schist on the faces of cliffs and in the boulders that litter the forests. The gneiss and schist are thought to have formed 2.75 billion years ago, when they were converted to more or less their present form from even older layers of sedimentary and volcanic rock that had been laid down on an ancient seabed. Eventually, these layers were buried under rock five to ten miles deep. There, under intense pressure and softened by heat in the neighborhood of a thousand degrees Fahrenheit, the layers warped, folded, twisted, and slowly churned. Geologists often call this chaotic blend of gneisses and schists "basement rocks" because they're similar to the rocks that underlie the continents.

The granitic portions of the Teton core oozed into place about 500 million years later. They rose as molten magma from deep inside the earth and melted their way into the gneisses and schists. As the magma cooled, it crystallized into an irregular mass of fine-grained granite shot through with a lacework of pegmatite, a coarse-grained rock very similar to granite. These veins of granite and pegmatite stretch across cliffs of dark gneiss like the cracks of a broken windshield. You can't see them from Signal Mountain, it's too far away. But you can see a dark, vertical stripe running down the east face of Mount Moran. That stripe—150 feet wide—is a column of diabase, a rock very similar to basalt, that was injected into the core as molten rock about a billion years after the granitic intrusion.

Geologists know the diabase squeezed into the core 1.3 billion years ago. They also know that the earliest layer of stone now capping the core formed roughly 600 million years ago. That leaves 700 million years unaccounted for. What happened? No one really knows. Perhaps no other rock layers at all were deposited. Or if they were, perhaps they were carried off by erosion. It's a mystery still waiting for a solution. (All those with theories about Topless Amazon Space Alien Miners, here's your big chance.) What is known is that the great mass of the Teton core itself was uplifted—cause unknown—during this time, exposed to erosion, and gradually smoothed into a vast, nearly featureless plain.

Then came the seas, a half billion years' worth of seas that washed across the future site of the Teton Range and indeed across much of what would become the western United States. The inundation began roughly 600 million years ago, at the close of Precambrian time, when primitive animals such as jellyfish represented the leading edge of evolution. As the waters came and went, they deposited vast sheets of sedimentary rock over the Teton core—miles of sandstone, limestone, dolomite, and shale.

A lot can happen in 500 million years, and the rock layers offer intriguing glimpses of the Teton area's distant past—of vast sand beaches and limestone headlands battered by storm waves. Of mucky tidal flats dried and cracked by the sun. Of quiet estuaries, coral reefs, masses of blue-green algae, and windblown sand. The rocks record fluctuations of climate and the veritable explosion of plant and animal life that spread from sea to land. At times, the Teton area lay beneath deep, clear seas. At other times it bore a strong resemblance to the Everglades—hot, humid, marshy, overgrown with lush vegetation. Simple, worm-like creatures wriggled in the mud, and an abundance of shell-bearing marine animals, such as clams and snails, littered the sea floor. There were trilobites and fish, reptiles and amphibians —even dinosaurs, perhaps including triceratops.

Most of what accumulated during those long years has eroded from the Teton Range, but perhaps the most striking remainder is the layer of Madison limestone that cloaks the north and south ends of the Tetons as well as the range's western slopes. Hundreds of feet thick and crammed with marine fossils, it forms high, vertical cliffs such as those that ring Alaska Basin, and it confronts day hikers with the enigmatic vista of a seabed draped across the peaks.

The explanation for how that seabed reached such rarefied heights can be traced far to the west, to a massive collision between the North American continent and the floor of the Pacific Ocean. Geologists believe North America separated from Europe about 200 million years ago and began moving westward as the Atlantic Ocean widened. As the

The Tetons began punching through the earth's surface just 8 to 10 million years ago, but the core of the range is composed of ancient metamorphic rock estimated to be 2.7 billion years old.

BENEVOLENT VANDALISM: GLACIAL CARVING

The spacious canyons that separate most of the Tetons' spectacular peaks were hollowed out by glaciers that formed at the crest of the range and followed the courses of streams downward. The streams had cut narrow, twisting gorges into the flanks of the mountains, and the glaciers widened and straightened those routes.

Glaciers begin to form wherever snowfall exceeds melting. As the layer of snow thickens, pressure converts the snow into hard, blue ice, which begins to flow plastically when it reaches depths of roughly one hundred feet. Continually replenished with snowfall, the glacier flows downward, picking up loose boulders, stones, and gravel, yanking others from the walls of the canyon, and pushing the whole abrasive mass along like a giant belt sander in slow motion.

The glacier will extend itself until its leading edge merges with another glacier or arrives in a climate warm enough to stop its advance. Even then, however, the glacier continues to churn away, burrowing itself deeper and deeper into the trough it occupies.

continent moved westward, it collided with and overrode the floor of the Pacific. The land crumpled, like a fender bender in slow motion. The continent's basement rocks cracked. Mountains were heaved upward and valleys formed. As the sea floor dove under the continent, portions of it melted and bubbled upward through the continental crust. Volcanoes erupted, and enormous slabs of rock—big enough to qualify as mountain ranges—broke free and slid for dozens of miles across the surface of the land.

This titanic disruption gradually moved inland and began heaving up the Rocky Mountains about 65 million years ago during a general uplift known as the Laramide Orogeny. Except for the Tetons, most of the mountains that surround Jackson Hole were built during this time. The Snake River Range slid into place at the south end of the valley as a great overthrust block of sedimentary rock. To the east, the Gros Ventre Mountains rose in place as a hump of Precambrian basement rocks that lifted and warped overlying layers of sedimentary rocks. The Washakie Range, to the northeast, is another block of basement rock, but that one was shoved west and then buried under thousands of feet of volcanic debris. Though the Tetons as we know them did not form for another 50 million years or so, the core of the range did rise several thousand feet during the Laramide Orogeny along what would become the general trend of the modern range.

As all of these mountains rose, streams and rivers formed and began stripping away the thousands of feet of sedimentary rock that had been laid down over the course of hundreds of millions of years. Much of the debris washed into the basin that would become Jackson Hole. Then, starting about 40 to 45 million years ago, volcanoes in the Yellowstone-Absaroka area spewed lava and ash over the region's basins and mountains.

* * *

From my perch at the Jackson Point Overlook, I troll through the geologists' accounts of the distant past and try to imagine what this place looked like before the Teton Range blocked the view to the west. But it's a vain, abstract attempt. The subterranean churning, the warp and heave, the accumulation and uplift—none of it builds a landscape, at least not in my dull noggin. I just can't blink away that great sweeping wall of broken rock and somehow blend its absence with the far more sedate view of dark foothills spilling off into the west from my own home on the Idaho side of the range. No. For me, today, this cresting wave of granite, gneiss, and schist has been here forever, poised above the sagebrush since the dawn of time.

Which is ridiculous. Because the Tetons, geologically speaking, formed in the very recent past. In spite of their ancient core, they are the youngest range in Wyoming—mere striplings, still in the midst of a growth spurt.

They began punching through the earth's crust 8 to 10 million years ago, but the process that created them was quite different from the great fender bender that pushed up the neighboring ranges. The Tetons rose as the result of just the opposite sort of movement.

THE FAULT ZONE

Cutting across the lower flank of Rockchuck Peak, a sixty-foot fault scarp records slippage between the floor of Jackson Hole and the abrupt, eastern flank of the Tetons. It's part of a major fault zone that built—and continues to build—the Tetons.

All along the fault zone, two great masses of rock grind against each other. One of them, the mountain core, rises. The other, the valley floor, sinks. Over the course of some 8 to 10 million years, the two bodies of rock have separated roughly five vertical miles. The main reason we see just six thousand feet of vertical is that erosion has stripped most of the sedimentary rock that once lay on top of the Tetons. Continuing movement along the fault explains why no foothills obscure the eastern flank of the range.

Movement comes intermittently and in the company of earthquakes large and small. On average, the rock masses have separated four inches each century. Geologists say the Jackson Hole area is overdue for a major quake.

That is, they formed as the earth's crust was pulled apart. As the crust separated, the floor of Jackson Hole—the entire vast plain—began to sink, tilting westward toward the emerging Teton Range. Meanwhile, the Teton core heaved upward, bearing a thick cap of sedimentary layers. These two great masses of rock moved against one another on what geologists call a fault zone— a series of deep, hairline cracks in the ground that stretch along the base of the Teton Range.

Movement came in fits and starts to the accompaniment of earthquakes, some major, some minor, each one marking another grinding slip along the fault zone. Over the course of millions of years, the two bodies of rock have separated by an astonishing distance. The mile-long, full-gainer with a half-twisting free fall from the summit of Mount Moran into Jackson Lake doesn't begin to cover the gap between the slabs. You'd have to burrow another twenty-four thousand feet beneath the surface of the valley floor before you could touch the sandstone layer that corresponds with a thin veneer of the same stuff on top of Mount Moran. Total displacement, then, is about thirty thousand feet. With that kind of free fall, a 150-pound skydiver could plunge the void for about 210 seconds before pulling his chute.

From Signal Mountain, you can easily see where the fault zone lies. Just trace the western edge of the valley floor, where it laps against the meandering base of the Teton Range. You have to get closer to the mountains to see the fault scarps, which record slippage between the valley and mountain bodies of rock. A scarp often appears as a horizontal scar following the contour of a slope. You can see one on the flank of Rockchuck Peak from the Cathedral Group Turnout on Jenny Lake Road.

Continuing movement along the fault zone explains why no foothills obscure the steep eastern slopes of the Tetons. And the reason we see a mere six to seven thousand spectacular feet of vertical is, of course, that most of the sedimentary rocks that capped the Tetons have been stripped away by erosion. Also, as the valley floor dropped, all manner of debris piled in on top of it. Rocks, sand, silt, dirt, boulders, pebbles, gravel, volcanic ash—cubic miles of the accumulated stuff, most of it hacked from the surrounding mountains by erosion and dumped there by running water and huge glaciers.

The fault zone that runs along the base of the Teton Range marks the eastern-most extension of the Teton Basin and Range—a region of narrow mountain ranges separated by broad, flat valleys that is usually associated with the landscapes of Nevada and Utah. Throughout this region, the earth's crust is being pulled apart. The cause? In part, a hot spot in the earth's mantle—a vast upwelling of molten magma that has been melting the overlying crust for millions of years. No one really knows why the hot spot developed. One intriguing, and controversial, theory suggests that a huge meteorite slammed into the ground between Idaho and Oregon about 16 to 18 million years ago, cracking the crust and creating the hot spot. Whatever its origin, the hot spot might have been sufficient eventually to split North America. But because the continent continues to move westward, the hot spot merely stretches

At sunrise, Mount Moran looms over Grassy Island in Jackson Lake.

the crust. Over the years, the hot spot has melted a long smear across the land from Boise to Yellowstone. That smear is the Snake River Plain, and the hot spot now lies beneath Yellowstone, where it has had a far greater impact on the landscape than simply heating up water for the geysers.

Three times in the past 1.8 million years, Yellowstone has blown its top in massive calderic explosions that make the eruptions of Mount St. Helens, Krakatoa, and Vesuvius seem as insignificant as a deer mouse breaking wind. To grasp the incredible violence of the explosion, imagine an irregular circle some thirty by fifty miles in diameter—a three-day hike across—suddenly detonating, all of it at once, disintegrating and spewing the entire region with ash, lava, and other debris.

* * *

A tidy veneer of grass, wildflowers, shrubs, and evergreen forest mask much of the Teton area's violent, earth-wrenching past. But the effects of glaciation remain vividly exposed. They are easy to pick out from our Signal Mountain vantage point. Spacious canyons separating the peaks are U-shaped troughs hollowed out by alpine glaciers flowing down to the valley. The Grand Teton is a horn chiseled by glaciers gnawing at it from three sides. Some of the peaks have long, knife-edged crests that were formed by glaciers working both sides of the ridgeline. The spectacular, bowl-shaped cirques of the high country were scooped out by glaciers. And the tract of dimpled land to the southwest, called The Potholes, formed when glacial ice chunks trapped beneath outwash debris melted. Although about a dozen glaciers continue to nibble away at the highest peaks, they are not remnants of Ice Age glaciers. Geologists think these tiny ice sheets formed sometime in the past one thousand years.

The real work of carving out the Tetons was done by immense bodies of ice that plowed into the valley perhaps ten times during the past million years. Because each ice advance tended to obliterate evidence of the last, scientists can reconstruct little except what happened during two relatively recent glaciations. During each period, alpine glaciers formed along the spine of the Tetons and flowed toward the valley, where some of them joined a much larger mass of ice moving down from the north, northeast, or east. During the first glaciation, 140,000 to 160,000 years ago, this colossal body of ice filled the entire valley, sometimes to depths of 4,000 feet. It slid right over Signal Mountain and pushed one lobe down into Hoback Canyon and another toward Fall Creek to the southwest. It overrode and streamlined buttes on the valley floor, polishing their sides and summits—Blacktail Butte, near Moose, is one of them. The ice melted away completely about 125,000 years ago.

The second major glaciation scientists can reconstruct started 40,000 to 70,000 years ago and came in three phases. The ice flowed in from three different directions, but never advanced farther than the northern end of the valley. During these phases, moraines were deposited on the valley floor, The Potholes were created, and a river of melting ice flowed

I mmense glaciers during at least two separate ice ages carved the Tetons into the familiar landscape we admire today. Here, they stand over the rich wetlands of Blacktail Ponds, which developed behind beaver dams and provide habitat for moose and waterbirds.

BRAIDED CHANNELS

Where it flows along the base of the Tetons, the Snake River is an unruly, changeable beast that twists from one side of its channel to the next. During high water, the Snake can be hundreds of yards wide—strong and purposeful. At low water, the current seems to lose its direction among gravel islands and channels which are sometimes blocked by logjams. The result is a pattern normally associated with quick-moving rivers, mobile streambeds, and weak banks. The Snake's shifting bed of rounded gravel and glacial cobbles rolls around too much to form stable channels. Farther downstream, where it enters its hard-walled canyon, the river does not change noticeably from one year to the next.

MOUNTAIN BUILDING

The Tetons began to break through the earth's surface 8 to 10 million years ago, which makes them the youngest mountain range in Wyoming. And yet, they are composed of some of the oldest rocks on the planet.

Their creation story begins nearly 3 billion years ago, as intense pressure and heat deep within the earth blended and utterly changed layers of ancient sedimentary stone into a mass of swirled metamorphic rocks. This mass of gneiss and schist was later invaded by an immense infusion of granite and, later still, by vertical injections of diabase. These rocks form the core of the Tetons.

Between 100 and 600 million years ago, a thick cap of sedimentary rock formed over the Teton core as seas advanced and retreated throughout the region.

All of these rocks were heaved upward about 65 million years ago during a general mountain-building phase called the Laramide Orogeny. Geologists trace the uplift to a gradual collision between the North American continent and the floor of the Pacific Ocean. The collision crumpled the western margin of the continent and helped build the mountains that neighbor the Tetons.

Rocks composing the central core of the Tetons are often called "basement rocks" because they resemble those which underlie the continents. In the Tetons, the basement rises to the very roof of the world.

The Teton Range is littered with tarns—tiny, deep lakes that occupy basins scooped out by glaciers. The same glaciers also formed cirques of cliffs above the water like the one that formed Indian Lake at 9,805 feet.

The Tetons themselves formed much later and as the result of a totally different process. Instead of rising as the earth's crust compressed, the Tetons rose as the earth's crust was pulled apart. Whatever the distant cause of that crustal extension may be, the rocks of the Teton core separated along the Teton Normal Fault. The block underlying the valley floor sank while the block that is now the Tetons rose.

Erosion stripped away most of the overlying layers of sedimentary rock, and at least two major periods of glaciation carved the ancient core of gneiss, schist, and granite into today's familiar profile of the Teton Range.

Covered by snow in winter, vast talus slopes lie beneath the peaks, formed by rocks that have fallen from the cliffs above.

The Grand Teton, like its immediate neighbors, is composed of a mass of fine-grained Precambrian granite shot through with quartz veins and pegmatite dikes.

Frost-sharpened spires stud the upper flanks of Teewinot Mountain.

Hidden here by Teewinot Mountain, Teton Glacier is one of several small, alpine glaciers that still shape the peaks. None of today's glaciers are remnants of the last ice age. Geologists think they may have formed as recently as 800 years ago.

through the valley, carving the series of stairstepping river terraces we see today. Several alpine glaciers also reached the valley floor, where they deposited the moraines that help form Leigh, Jenny, Bradley, Taggart, and Phelps lakes. The last of the ice from this second glaciation melted away 12,000 to 15,000 years ago.

* * *

We tend to think of geology as stuff that happened in the unimaginably distant past, and yet there is a vivid reminder in the Teton area that the landscape remains restless. On the east side of Jackson Hole, there is a long scar on the face of Sheep Mountain where 50 million cubic yards of rock, soil, and forest broke loose on June 26, 1925. In just three minutes, the slide ripped a gash one mile long, a half mile wide, and nearly two hundred feet deep. The slurry of mud, boulders, trees, and gravel surged across the Gros Ventre River, ran 400 feet up the opposite slope, and built a dam 2,000 feet wide and 225 to 250 feet high. This dam held for almost two years, then burst, releasing a flood that killed six people and left forty families homeless. Lower Slide Lake is a remnant of the larger lake.

Geologists say a minor earthquake probably touched off the Gros Ventre Slide. Such earthquakes are common along the fault zones that surround Jackson Hole. Many are so slight we do not feel them, but every now and then one wakes up the town. These little earthquakes—along with wind, the freeze-thaw cycle, and the constant hydraulic pressure of rivers and streams—continue to shape the land in subtle ways. But there are, perhaps, more dramatic catastrophes in the offing. What would a truly massive earthquake do to the valley with so many homes built along the fault zones, and with so much of Jackson Lake's water held back by a dam also on the fault zone? Some think the Big One's overdue.

And then there's that curious hot spot up in Yellowstone. Geologists say all the ingredients for another calderic explosion are in place—a huge mass of molten magma lies just a few thousand feet below the surface. And the timing's right. Yellowstone has blown its lid at intervals of about six hundred thousand years. The last one came about six hundred thousand years ago. So, give or take ten thousand years, we're about due for the Really Big One.

Sure would unsnarl a few traffic jams up there.

Cascade Canyon is an outstanding example of how a large mountain glacier has straightened, deepened, and steepened the walls of a narrow, stream-eroded valley.

Jenny Lake is impounded by a moraine pushed into place by the glaciers that carved out Cascade Canyon.

Out in the waist-high brush, on the cusp of dawn, the turpentine tang of sage hangs in the damp, cool air. Across the flat floor of the valley, the Tetons rise against a dark blue sky still pierced by scattered stars. I amble along, threading my way between the big shrubs, side-stepping prickly pear cactus and admiring the tiny buds of wild blue flax that have closed up shop for the night. Soon, a crease of golden light catches the crest of the range and works its way down, warming the cliffs and canyons, the rocky knobs and spires, the snowfields, the broad band of evergreen forests, and finally, the floor of the valley itself. The powder blue petals of the flax slowly unwind and turn to the sun. Long shadows extend from every blade of grass, every twig of sagebrush, and tiny wildflowers—in crimson, purple, yellow, and blue—burst against the tangled backdrop of pale green.

I hate rolling out of bed so early in the morning, but this is by far the park's finest hour. At no time are the colors richer, the shadows deeper, or the light more flattering to the famous profile of the Tetons' eastern front. The deer and elk have not yet retreated to the forests, and most of the park's visitors have not yet emerged from their sleeping bags. In just a few hours, the rising sun will bleach much of the color from the land and simplify its contours by erasing the shadows. The wind will pick up, and so will the sounds of spinning

A crush of wildflowers blooms near Pass Lake. Color, fragrance, texture, shape: we regard these as aesthetic qualities, but to plants they reflect reproductive strategies.

EDEN ON AN INCLINE
PLANT LIFE OF THE TETONS

tires and the rumble of trucks, cars, RVs, and buses on the park's roads. But for now, there is only the drowsy beauty of the awakening land and a pervasive stillness broken only by the cheerful nattering of birds.

Suddenly, a loud, whirring buzz whips past my ear, and I see a hummingbird streak across the sagebrush at twigtop level, then dive into the brush just a few feet away. It's after scarlet gilia this morning, a tall prairie plant with bright red, trumpet-shaped flowers. The bird hovers from blossom to blossom, inserting its long bill and licking nectar from the flowers with its monofilament tongue. Then it rises, checks traffic, and darts away, probably to another scarlet gilia, where it will inadvertently brush off the pollen it has picked up here and bring to a climax the gilial equivalent of sexual intercourse.

When we look at plants—whether they grow here on the floor of Jackson Hole, in meadows beneath the high cliffs, or in our own backyards—we tend to think of them as stationary objects, passive at best. They sprout and grow in the same spot, wait politely for the arrival of hummingbirds and various insects, reproduce if given the chance, then shut down for the season. And they never complain—not when a moose clips their twigs, not when a logging truck rumbles past with a few of their amputated chums laid out for the sawmill. And so we often think of plants as just being there when in fact they are dynamic, highly adaptable organisms capable of reacting to sudden changes in their surroundings.

For example, as the sun rises this morning and dries out the floor of Jackson Hole, sagebrush all over the valley will close microscopic pores under their leaves in order to conserve moisture. And, at specific intervals throughout the day, various flowers will open their petals, rev up their nectaries, and release their seductive smells. Some will close for the night as males and open the next morning as females.

Plants also react to events with longer-range consequences. When fire sweeps through a forest of subalpine fir and Engelmann spruce, sun-loving wildflowers, shrubs, aspen, and lodgepole pine reclaim the ground. When spring floods cave in river banks and topple old trees, narrowleaf cottonwood and willow pioneer the new gravel bars. Avalanches, landslides, windstorms, earthquakes, broad-scale climate changes, overgrazing by cattle and wildlife, insects, disease, the upheaval of mountains, the industrious exertions of beavers and pocket gophers—all these and many other influences force plants to react.

Some of the most fascinating reactions are best viewed over the long haul of evolution and often involve reproductive strategies. Take scarlet gilia and the hummingbird's beak. Each evolved its specialized structures in response to the other, the changes accruing incrementally over successive generations. The result is a flower that reserves its nectar for the hummer, and a bird that so prefers the flower that it can be depended upon to ferry pollen between individuals of the same species.

Besides hummingbirds, Grand Teton's plants depend on many different insects

Yellow columbine thrives among rockslides and stony outcrops, but it also does well in ravines and in the shade of aspen groves. Its relative, the blue columbine, loses its vivid color the farther west and north one travels from Colorado.

to attend to their sex lives. Some flowers have evolved as veritable punch bowls of pollen, with their petals flung open for any beetle, fly, bee, moth, or butterfly who cares to crash the party. But this strategy invites all manner of insect revelers, many of whom may overstay their welcome or fail to carry their burdens of pollen to another individual plant of the same species.

Other flowers specialize in order to attract a few faithful pollinators and keep the barbarians at the gate. They bloom in colors especially alluring to their preferred pollinators and sport specialized structures that accommodate the mouthparts or bodies of specific insects. Still others open for business only when their pollinators are active. And so, some are thought of as bee flowers, others as bird flowers, a few as wasp flowers, and still others as moth or butterfly flowers.

Many of Grand Teton's plants throw their sex lives to the wind, indiscriminately dusting the entire surface of the park with pollen in the hopes that, say, lodgepole pollen will bond with lodgepole stigma rather than with the aluminum roof of a motor home. While the process of wind pollination may strike us as haphazard, the chances of success are rather good. Clover, for instance, produces six thousand grains of pollen for every available clover stigma. Cheerful odds, if you happen to be female.

Still other plants abandon sex entirely and reproduce vegetatively, as clones. Aspen trees usually reproduce this way in the Tetons, and so do many plants that must survive in the brutal climate at or above treeline.

* * *

If you stand on the floor of Jackson Hole for a while and gaze over the valley at the Tetons, you begin to notice that the plants have arranged themselves in distinct communities. Sagebrush, grass, and prairie wildflowers stretch across the flats for miles, interrupted here and there by a few stray limber pines and some isolated stands of lodgepole. Meandering ribbons of cottonwood trees and thick underbrush mark the course of the Snake and Gros Ventre Rivers. And dense evergreen forests rise along the flanks of the Tetons, thinning toward the crest of the range and then giving out entirely.

From a distance, the boundaries seem clear-cut and closely tied to elevation. The higher you go, the more brutal the climate. Average temperatures drop, and the growing season shortens. More rain and snow falls in the high country, but evaporative rates increase due to greater wind speeds and more intense sunlight. All of this profoundly affects the distribution of plants, but changes in elevation don't explain everything. After all, the grassy slopes of the Gros Ventre foothills lie at the same elevation as the dense mountain forests directly across the valley. And in the mountain forests themselves, the intermingling of tree and other plant species cannot be accounted for by elevation alone.

Topography, or the shape of the land, is another factor. The wall-like presence of the Tetons themselves deprives Jackson Hole of rain and snow by clawing much of the moisture

A sparse covering of alpine wildflowers make a go of it in rocky soil above treeline at Fox Creek Pass. Compared to the alpine climate, the arctic summer seems balmy, benign.

oisture drains
quickly through the
porous soils on the floor
of Jackson Hole, pro-
moting the growth of
prairie and desert
plants that can cope
with water stress.

from passing storms and funneling the water back to Idaho. The canyons of the Tetons can depress the treeline hundreds of feet by draining cold air from the high country. The ravines, gullies, and creases that lace the Gros Ventre foothills channel moisture into aspen groves. And dry, south-facing slopes support different types of plants than do cooler, north-facing slopes right across the gully. The shifts in vegetation are often abrupt, and the contrast between plant types stark and extreme—grass and prickly pear cactus one moment, an aspen grove thick with Richardson geraniums the next.

When all other factors seem equal, soil type takes a hand. The most dramatic examples are the stands of lodgepole pine that rise like islands from the sagebrush flats of Jackson Hole. The pines grow on glacial moraines, where clay in the soil holds moisture. But water percolates quickly through the gravelly soils of the valley floor, surrendering the field to sagebrush and plants of the prairies and deserts.

Even though the boundaries blur on closer inspection, ecologists generally recognize five major plant communities in the Tetons: the riparian (or streamside community), the sagebrush steppe, the foothills, mountain forests, and the alpine.

* * *

The park's waterways stretch from the crest of the mountains to the floor of the valley. Beginning far above treeline, they slip down the rocky slopes from snowfields and wind along as tiny, glassine streams through subalpine meadows choked with wildflowers such as Columbia monkshood, mountain bluebells, and yellow monkeyflower. On the relatively flat, glaciated floors of the canyons, the water pools and soaks broad areas overgrown with nearly impenetrable thickets of willow and alder. The creeks spill from the mouths of canyons as frothing cascades and plunge into the forests below, where common self-heal and pink wintergreen grow along the shaded water's edge. Some flow into the morainal lakes that glimmer at the base of the Tetons. Others sweep across the semiarid floor of Jackson Hole and join the Snake or Gros Ventre Rivers, their swift waters nurturing ribbons of cottonwoods, aspen, blue spruce, and many different shrubs. Along the way, streams often stall out behind beaver dams and clots of fallen trees and shrubs. Or a stream may change its course during a spring flood and abandon a bend of its former route. That leaves a slough, a quiet backwater that often becomes a marsh. Oxbow Bend, just a few miles below Jackson Lake Dam, is one of these placid areas. Its still waters often reflect a classic view of the Tetons, and the ponds draw moose, otters, swans, osprey, bald eagles, herons, geese, and ducks.

Whether the water gurgles through a high, treeless meadow or laps politely at the edge of a pond, it supports a sinuous belt of vegetation quite different from the plants that grow just a few dozen feet from the water's edge. These riparian corridors, as they are often called, are essential to wildlife. They offer drinking water, of course, but also shelter and food in the form of lush grasses, forbs, broadleaf shrubs, and aquatic plants rich in carbohydrates.

Sun-loving fireweed blooms in an aspen meadow. To avoid self-pollination, fireweed's male and female parts ripen at different times.

Aspen, the most
widely distributed tree
in North America, sheds
its leaves in autumn
but remains capable of
photosynthesis through-
out the winter because
its bark contains
chlorophyll.

The most obvious riparian corridors in the park follow the courses of the Snake and Gros Ventre Rivers. These plant communities live in a healthy state of flux, constantly cycling between destruction and renewal. Spring floods tear at the banks, exposing the roots of trees and eventually toppling them. Shrubs get washed out. Banks cave in. The channel shifts. Gravel bars are swept away, then rebuilt. With each rainstorm, the water level rises and falls, and the velocity of the current fluctuates. Fires sometimes sweep the banks. The plants cope admirably with these sudden changes. Narrowleaf cottonwood is one of the first species to establish itself on newly created gravel and sand bars. Another cottonwood, black cottonwood, clads itself in a thick bark that helps protect it from fire. What we see of grasses and wildflowers may burn during a fire, but these plants have extensive root systems that quickly send up new shoots. If it weren't for flood, fire, and other disturbances, evergreens could establish a stronger foothold along the rivers and eventually crowd out cottonwoods and willows. Such a displacement could put pressure on moose and beaver, two animals that depend on cottonwoods and willows for food.

Plants growing in the warmer, slower, often shallower water of sloughs, beaver ponds, and other backwater areas include cattails, bulrushes, reeds, lilies, arum-leaf arrowhead, and common bladderwort, a stringy, murderous plant that traps and digests aquatic insects. Many of the marshy plants store starch in highly nutritious tubers, corms, and roots prized by diving ducks, geese, muskrats, and people. They also provide cover and nesting materials for shorebirds and waterfowl.

Grasses, sedges, shrubs, and wildflowers jam the moist soils surrounding the marshy areas. Here you'll find milkweed, a showy perennial with a ruthless sex life. Its pink, orange, and red blossoms pander to legions of insects. When a bug lands and forages for nectar, it trips a snare that attaches a special clip to its leg. The clip bears a small package of pollen. The bug is supposed to tear itself away from the flower and carry the pollen clip to another receptive milkweed. Bigger insects, such as butterflies and bumblebees, manage the task with little apparent difficulty. But small insects that tangle with the charms of milkweed may not be strong enough to pull themselves away. They die from exhaustion.

* * *

To the casual eye, the vast expanse of sagebrush covering the dry floor of Jackson Hole can seem dull, monotonous, boring. Like the old fella in the pickup says, "You seen a couple hundred thousand sagebrush, pard, you seen 'em all." But there's more to the place than an endless tangle of scraggly shrubs. For one thing, the scraggly shrubs themselves are a lot more interesting than they seem at first glance. For another, the sagebrush canopy masks a fascinating community of plants. Once you get out of the car and start walking, grasses smooth the going underfoot and an abundance of wildflowers perk things up—arrow-leaf balsamroot, blazing star mentzelia, showy goldeneye, lupine, and low larkspur, just to name a few.

Here, where the meadow death camas blooms, water stress is a way of life. Though the valley receives a generous amount of precipitation annually, its surface remains dry because it is filled to a depth of two thousand feet with sand, gravel, and cobblestones the size of melons. Moisture slips quickly past roots and rhizomes, and it evaporates quickly, too. Plants adapt in a variety of ways. Some have deep taproots. Many have leathery leaves or a waxy coating that slows evaporation. Others diffuse sunlight with fuzzy hairs. Sagebrush has a dual root system adapted to take advantage of the valley's two-stage precipitation profile. A shallow set of roots radiate from the plant to absorb the abundant moisture of spring and early summer. Other roots plunge deeply into the soil and serve the plant well during the long, dry months of July, August, and September.

In addition to arid conditions, plants of the sagebrush steppe must also put up with Jackson Hole's bitterly cold winters and relatively short growing season. Sagebrush is capable of cranking up its photosynthetic process on short notice so it can take advantage of a sunny day in January, for instance. It grows at temperatures close to freezing and also creates benevolent depressions for itself in the snow pack. Its relatively dark evergreen leaves act as passive solar collectors which warm in the winter sunlight, melt the snow, and hollow out depressions around each grizzled shrub. The depressions reduce windchill and collect more snow, which melts and moistens the soil. But there's a drawback. Because sagebrush is one of the few plants that protrude above the snow, it is an important winter food source for mule deer, elk, antelope, and grouse. The shrub's characteristic fragrance is due to volatile oils that may be a mild form of defense against these sometimes overindulgent herbivores.

* * *

Along the eastern fringe of Jackson Hole rise the grassy, rumpled foothills of the Gros Ventre Mountains and the Mount Leidy Highlands. The foothills here, as well as those along the gentle, west side of the Tetons, present plants and animals with a moderate climate, one that is generally warmer than that of the high mountains and wetter than that of the valley floor. The landscape shifts from an inclined version of the sagebrush steppe to grasslands, woodlands, and windswept ridges. The foothills are an important winter range for elk, deer, bighorn sheep, and antelope because food and shelter are close at hand. The lee slopes provide protection from storms and cover from predators, while windswept slopes offer the dried remains of the summer's bounty—bluebunch wheatgrass, needle-and-thread grass, serviceberry, and many other plants. Mule deer congregate in large herds during winter and are often seen pawing the thin snow cover or nibbling the brush on windswept and south-facing slopes.

Aspen, the most widespread tree in North America, grows throughout the park in moist depressions, ravines, and valley bottoms and on the slopes of ridges where snow tends to accumulate. But perhaps they are most noticeable here in the foothills, where the groves stand in abrupt contrast to the open, grassy slopes and where they glimmer each autumn with

BIG SAGEBRUSH: A NATURAL WATER PUMP

summer rains. When winter winds rake the high plains, sagebrush traps and holds snow. In this way it not only provides shelter but conserves moisture—instead of blowing away and evaporating, the snow melts into the ground.

By thriving where most other plants would die, sagebrush provides essential food and cover for a rich community of plants and animals. Living virtually secret lives beneath the sagebrush canopy are grasses, wildflowers, rodents, jackrabbits, sage grouse, sage sparrows, badgers, coyotes, and many others. More conspicuous are a few larger animals,

Sagebrush has a peculiar way of hiding in the landscape it dominates. Covering the floor of Jackson Hole—and much of the mountain West—its very numbers make it inconspicuous. Yet sage is an important and talented plant. Its taproot, growing five to six feet deep, allows it to drink deep when dry conditions parch the surface. It also has a network of shallow lateral roots to take advantage of light

notably pronghorn, who are at home among the sage in the way terns are at home on the sea.

No one who has breathed summer air scented by the aromatic oils of sage can ever forget the fragrance. Like the smell of the ocean, or of a pine woods, one whiff of sage can bring back old and vivid memories. It seems in character that the most distinctive property of this unassuming plant is an invisible one.

PLANT DIVERSITY

Though Grand Teton's plants divide into distinct communities, the boundaries often overlap, blur, and blend in complex ways. Elevation plays a key role in determining where plants tend to grow. The higher you go, the more brutal the climate. The growing season shortens, sunlight intensifies, evaporative rates increase, and average windspeeds accelerate. All of which adds up to a climate that's colder, drier (at least in the alpine), and more apt to snap tree limbs.

But the shape of the land, or topography, also has a profound influence on plant distribution. If a slope faces north, for example, it offers plants a cooler, moister environment than a slope that faces the sun all day. And cold air draining along the upper rim of a canyon can depress treeline by hundreds of feet. Soil type also affects where plants grow because some soils hold moisture better than others. The moraines on the floor of Jackson Hole retain moisture better than the gravelly flatlands around them. That's why evergreen forests grow on the moraines, surrounded by a sea of sagebrush.

Glacier lilies, also called dogtooth violets, grow abundantly above seventy-five hundred feet, blossoming along the receding snowline. Important forage for wildlife, glacier lilies are capable of growing through melting snow.

Elevation, topography, soil type. Taken together, these and other influences divide Teton's plants into five major communities: the riparian (or streamside), the sagebrush steppe, the foothills, mountain forests, and the alpine.

golden leaves. All the trees within a particular grove may turn color within days of one another, then drop their leaves in a single gusty afternoon. This is because most of the park's aspens, though capable of setting seed, tend to reproduce vegetatively. They send up shoots—clones, really—that grow into trees and form genetically uniform groves. In a sense, then, the grove can be viewed as a single, ancient plant rather than as a group of individuals. Its offshoots may live for a hundred years or so, but the plant itself may be thousands of years old—perhaps even dating back eleven thousand years to the late Pleistocene.

The foothills are a great place to wander aimlessly with a bug book in one hand and a field guide to wildflowers in the other. There are dozens of gorgeous blossoms, many of them dressed to the nines in order to charm the pollen off some exotic six-legged creature. With a little patience, you can begin to see method in the apparent madness of buzzing flight plans, and insects soon reveal themselves as more than things to swat. Along open slopes, I like to look for hot rock penstemon, a shrubby plant with lots of small, white, tubular flowers that have conspicuous purple lines inside the tube. The lines help guide insects to the flower's nectaries while the flower, if it's in the male stage, dusts the rummaging bug with pollen. If the flower is in its female stage, said bug will lodge pollen collected from a different penstemon on its stigma. Late in the day, you might come across yellow evening primrose—a tall, stiff plant loaded with delicate yellow blossoms. It opens its petals at night and closes them again at sunrise in order to preserve its nectar for hawkmoths, the nocturnal equivalent of hummingbirds.

* * *

Mountain forests blanket the steep eastern slopes of the Tetons, starting at the foot of the range and extending upward toward its crest. From the valley floor, the bands of forest look rather uniform—broad patches of dark green, interrupted here and there by massive shoulders of gray rock, meadows, or the steep ramps of boulder fields and avalanche chutes. But within each forest there is great diversity and a totally different feel from any other major ecozone in the park. Elsewhere, the sense of wide open country predominates. Vistas take in the entire Teton Range, the floor of the valley, miles of rumpled foothills, the glint of a distant windshield. But in the forest, with the surprising chill of its shadows and the smell of damp rock and soil in the air, the view often takes in little more than a few dozen yards. Sunlight slants through the trunks, dappling thickets of berry bushes. Wind sifts through the canopy; tree trunks creak and groan. Sometimes you walk beside a lazy stream, or past a waterfall, or out into a wildflower meadow with its sudden vista of high cliffs.

It's colder in the mountain forests than on the valley floor, much wetter, and the soil tends to be young, coarse, and rather lean on nutrients. Conifers here can withstand temperatures of minus seventy-six degrees Fahrenheit, and their needles, present year-round, can photosynthesize at or below freezing. This is a distinct advantage in a severe climate, and one the conifers enjoy over most, but not all, deciduous trees. Look carefully at an aspen trunk

Mountain ash grows in dense thickets along canyon streams. Moose heavily browse its twigs in winter, and grouse, cedar waxwings, grosbeaks, and bears eat its fruit.

FOLLOWING PAGES: Arrow-leaf balsam root, one of the most abundant wildflowers in the Tetons, can grow as high as two feet and sport flowers as large as four inches across. Elk and deer graze on the young shoots. Bighorn sheep prefer the leaves and flower heads.

sometime. You'll notice a distinct shade of green. That's chlorophyll in the bark, and it enables aspens to convert sunlight to food even after they drop their leaves.

The forests that stretch across the base of the Tetons consist mainly of lodge-pole pine. The tall, slender trunks grow in what seem to be ordered ranks on the moraines that impound the park's large lakes. Lodgepole is a pioneer species, a tree that tends to fill in gaps opened in forests by various disturbances, usually fires. It produces two types of cones, one of which is specially adapted to fire. Called a serotinous cone, it remains tightly closed until opened by intense heat. Then it releases abundant seeds, which fall into sunny mineral soils cleared of competing plants by the blaze. Because these cones must survive for many years while waiting for a convenient forest fire to justify their existence, they have to armor them-selves against marauding squirrels, which relish them. To discourage the squirrels, or at least to slow them down a bit, the cones are resinous, have sharp spines, and hang from branches in a way that's difficult for the rodents to get at. Once plucked, the dense cone is hard to crack. An interesting effect is that squirrels who live among lodgepole forests have developed larger jaw muscles than those living in, say, forests of Douglas fir, which produce softer cones.

Above the lodgepole forest, the east face of the Tetons supports broad expanses of subalpine fir and Engelmann spruce, with whitebark pine near the upper limit of the forests. These subalpine forests act as giant snowfences during winter and as immense refrigeration units during spring and early summer. Snow blowing off the scalp of the range accumulates in them, building to great depths and lingering into summer. The snow and shade of the dense canopy of trees depress average temperatures, shorten the growing season, and help retain moisture.

Engelmann spruce and subalpine fir predominate here because both do well in cold, moist, shady locations. In fact, subalpine fir is among the most shade-tolerant of all trees. Unlike lodgepole pine and Douglas fir, both species are capable of vegetative reproduction. When their lower branches are pressed to the ground by snow, the branches can produce roots and eventually become new trees. On average, Engelmann spruce live longer and grow larger than subalpine fir. The largest Engelmanns in the park are next to Hidden Falls; they have lived for more than four hundred years and stand eighty feet high, with trunk diameters of thirty-six inches.

* * *

As you hike into the highest regions of the park, the increasingly frigid, dry, and wind-hammering climate thins the trees and beats those that remain into tiny, twisted ver-sions of their relatives growing just a few hundred yards down the slopes. Some, called "banner trees," have been stripped of all their needles except those growing to leeward. Others huddle in thickets or behind large boulders, their branches deformed. Many of the subalpine firs barely qualify as modest Christmas trees, though some of these dwarfs have lived more than two hundred years. This strange and beautiful zone, often called "krummholz" (German for

A brush fire is only a memory amid the new growth and a lush carpet of grass and wildflowers.

The Snake River is the most obvious of the park's riparian corridors. Along its banks grow narrowleaf cottonwood, blue spruce, Engelmann spruce, Douglas fir, river birch, silver buffaloberry, and various willows.

"crooked wood"), is the forest's last gasp, a transition zone at the fringe of the treeless alpine regions of the park.

Treeline is determined primarily by temperature. At some point, it simply gets too cold for plants to manufacture enough of the carbon-rich compounds required for woody growth. But there are other factors, too. Winter winds dry out trees when water is unavailable because it is frozen on and under the ground. Deep snow can discourage tree growth, as can soils that are too wet, too dry, or too thin. So treeline in the Tetons varies greatly, but it generally fluctuates around ninety-five hundred feet.

Some treeline conifers cope with the cold by growing their leaves in dense clusters. The clusters maintain temperatures as much as ten degrees centigrade warmer than the surrounding air by creating a shield against the wind and presenting a larger surface to the sun's warmth. Dwarf subalpine firs often accumulate in protective knee-high thickets that act as windbreaks. A thicket begins as a single seedling, which establishes itself in the shelter of a boulder or a depression. As it grows, it hugs the ground and spreads to leeward, setting roots where its branches touch the soil, each new branch or clone shielding the next from the brutal wind. Given time, the plant can extend over a relatively large area. In effect, the thickets are trees that grow horizontally. And, because the windward edge of each thicket tends to die while the leeward edge extends itself, it may not be too romantic a notion to suggest that these trees actually migrate over the landscape.

* * *

Above treeline the alpine ecosystem sprawls over an expansive and extraordinarily diverse landscape. Soaring walls of glaciated rock and vast boulder fields cover much of the terrain, and they are bare of vegetation of any kind except for lichens. Other areas remain perpetually buried by persistent snowfields or glaciers. Where soil exists, alpine plants grow in lush meadows, willow thickets, sedge bogs, and—sparsely—on gravelly ridgetops.

These tiny plants eke out a living in a ferocious climate that is often held up as some sort of rough equivalent of the Arctic. But such a comparison understates the brutality of alpine conditions. There are, of course, some striking similarities—the bitter cold, the short growing season, the lack of trees, and the presence of many of the same wildflowers. However, while nearly endless days and steady temperatures bless the Arctic summer, the alpine is plagued by wildly fluctuating temperatures, shorter days, far more intense sunlight, higher rates of evaporation, and the persistent threat of drought. If alpine plants were tourists, boosters from the Arctic would send them travel brochures bragging up the balmy pleasures of life along the Bering Strait. But there are no charter buses leaving the alpine reaches of the Tetons, so the plants there have no choice but to tough it out in a cold, often desertlike environment—a supremely fragile ecosystem, easily damaged, slow to recover.

To avoid the worst of the weather, and to conserve moisture and warmth, alpine plants hug the ground. Their small size also reduces their need for nutrients and photo-synthesis. They concentrate most of their biomass underground in extensive root systems that store carbohydrates over the long winter and fuel the rapid growth of new leaves and stems the following spring. Annuals, which must start each year from seed, are rare. Some, such as glacier lilies, cheat the season by growing right through the snow. Many alpine flowers can grow in temperatures barely above thirty-two degrees and carry on photosynthesis in far colder conditions than their low-elevation counterparts. Many also contain anthocyanins, chemicals capable of warming plant tissue by converting sunlight into heat.

In some alpine areas, plants must deal with arid conditions as well as bitter cold. Winter winds may strip these areas of snow, leaving little or nothing to melt in the spring. Or, the soil may be so gravelly that water drains quickly past the roots. Some plants conserve moisture by growing as compact cushions. Others sink deep taproots. Moss campion does both. Its tiny pink flowers grow from a small, emerald green mat that looks like a patch of moss. The tightly woven mat, which attaches to a deep taproot, not only conserves moisture but warms the plant by acting as a windbreak and solar collector. Mountain townsendia diffuses intense sunlight with hairy leaves. Arctic willow slows evaporation with thick, leathery leaves.

The ferocious alpine climate that forces plants to make these and other adaptations also demands, at the very least, respect and prudence from human beings. Especially from dull-witted, teenage human beings. Years ago, I spent the better part of an adolescent summer at or above treeline, bombing around with a backpack, catching trout, worrying about Bigfoot and sometimes climbing high cliffs without benefit of ropes or brains. I remember one stormy afternoon in a tent, playing cribbage with a fellow immortal, while the sky opened up on us with heavy rain, then sleet, then hail. We had camped several hundred feet below a bare ridgeline and well away from the only tree—a large, isolated whitebark pine.

As we moved our pegs around the board, thunder caromed off the cliffs. We grinned at each other: cool! Then came an incredible flash, and in the immediate explosion I opened my eyes and saw Greg dropping back onto the floor of the tent. We hit at the same moment, unhurt, then scrambled outside. A long, ragged gash cut across the meadow's surface, passing within yards of the tent. There was the smell of smoke in the air, curious bits of black-ened wood among the damp wildflowers and melting hailstones, and farther along, more jagged cracks in the ground. Some of them were a hundred yards long, six inches deep, and had fresh dirt and cobbles thrown off to the sides. All of them radiated from a central point, and though we should have understood immediately, it took a few moments before we recognized the stump and remaining mangled limb of the whitebark pine. It also took us a few minutes to recognize that our tent, and indeed our own heads, were the highest points left on the meadow. Clearly it was time for us to adapt. We broke camp and hurried down the ridge.

Near Pilgrim Creek, a field of arrow-leaf balsamroot stretches out toward a stand of evergreens and the Tetons.

It's autumn, and we came to this broad meadow at the base of the Tetons about an hour before sunset. We've been sitting here in the open, concealed by the high brown grass, listening to dozens of restless elk in the surrounding forest of lodgepole pine. When dusk falls, they will emerge from the treeline, and we'll be able to watch the rut. But for now, there are only sounds. The hollow clatter of antlers. The thud of hooves on the run. The snap of breaking branches. Now and then, one of the bulls sends up a prolonged and eerie squeal that sails out over the meadow before tumbling into a series of hoarse grunts and bellows. This "bugling," as it is lamely called, is a demonstration of the bull's strength, vigor, and virility. It is a lure to cows, an open challenge to other bulls, and to human ears at least, a frank expression of sheer randiness unrivaled by any other animal in the Rockies.

Grand Teton's elk herd consists of about fifteen thousand animals, half of which pass the winter on the National Elk Refuge at the south end of Jackson Hole. There, they feed on grasses, forbs, and other natural vegetation. After the natural forage thins, a supplemental feeding program kicks in with pelletized alfalfa. The feeding is necessary because two-thirds of the herd's traditional winter range is now occupied by about ten thousand people.

In the spring, the elk move north off the sagebrush flats, following the retreating snowline and fanning out into the high country of the Tetons, the Gros Ventres, and the Yellowstone

A bull elk steps through a meadow during the autumn rut. Growing and bearing the added weight of antlers requires a greater diversion of nutrients and energy for bulls than pregnancy and lactation does for cows.

ALL ONE BREATH
ANIMAL COMMUNITIES

Plateau. Individual cows separate from their groups to give birth. Each licks its calf clean and eats the afterbirth as well as the soil and leaf litter from the birth site in order to conceal the scent of vulnerability from predators. The speckled calf hides on the sun-dappled forest floor while its mother grazes nearby. She will attack small predators such as coyotes and try to lure away more serious threats such as grizzly bears or cougars. After about three weeks, the calf is strong enough to join the herd.

By midsummer, many of the elk move about seventy miles north of Jackson, where they graze on bunchgrass in high meadows along the Continental Divide. They gain strength and weight all summer in preparation for the coming winter and, in the case of bulls, for the impending strain of the autumn rut.

And the rut is an arduous rite indeed, at least for the bulls.

As the light fades across our meadow, small groups of nonchalant cows step into the open. Soon, a bull trots out of the forest, hurrying to get ahead of his harem. His neck is stretched far forward, his head held steady and low, his immense rack of antlers silhouetted against the pale sky. He pauses, his lips part, and when the wrenching squeal ends in that abrupt series of grunts we see his belly contract with every *uhng-uhng-uhng*. He's challenging a rival we can't see. Yet.

This bull has arrived on the mating scene with something every other bull who has any hope of attracting a harem must have—a burdensome but eye-catching rack of antlers. Producing the requisite equipment is no trivial matter. Biologists estimate that growing and carrying antlers requires a greater diversion of nutrients and energy than does pregnancy and lactation. A good rack, then, is proof of a bull's vigor, proof of its ability to provide well for itself. Cows seem to understand that. No rack, no whoopie.

Our bull keeps bugling, and we reach for our sweaters as the chill comes on and a few stars appear. Some nights you see very little of the action because it gets too dark, and all you can do is listen and imagine. But tonight we're in luck. The rival steps warily over a rise in the meadow, and in the half light, we can see that he's another magnificent bull. After some preliminary posturing, the two animals approach one another and lower their heads. We hear the antlers clatter as they make some tentative thrusts and parries. Then the racks lock together, and they begin a shoving match. Their hooves kick up dust. They wheel for advantage, occasionally part, then rejoin.

On other evenings, we've watched rutting bulls sap their strength in other ways—raking their antlers against tree trunks, pawing the ground, running off upstart bulls, and herding groups of willing females. They also hose themselves down with their own urine— soaking their bellies, faces, and manes—then strut around in a steaming mist laced with reproductive hormones. Once wet, they often roll in the dust and cake themselves in a fragrant mudpack. All this to attract a bevy of six to twenty choosy but admiring cows who consent to

A beaver strips bark, its dietary staple, from an aspen branch. The labors of these stout mammals affect the ecosystem far beyond filling their needs for food and shelter. Their dams prevent erosion, sustain consistent streamflows during summer and, over centuries, can even trap enough sediment to create flat mountain meadows in what might otherwise have been steeply sloping valleys.

THE ELUSIVE OTTER

Tenacious hunters, otters pursue a wide variety of prey, sometimes with surprising ingenuity. Fast and agile underwater, they dive for fish, grub the muck for frogs, and rummage the banks for small mammals and birds. But they also have been known to tear apart beaver dams and then bound into the diminished pond to gorge on trapped fish and frogs. They launch submerged attacks on ducks and other waterbirds, and they will pursue muskrats and even beavers into their burrows and lodges and kill them. Few predators, on the other hand, have a chance to catch this almost completely aquatic mammal, but coyotes sometimes manage to surprise them on land.

mate, linger for a time, and then trot off, presumably refreshed, for their winter range. Meanwhile, the bulls—much depleted by their exertions and made conspicuous by their heavy antlers—are often targeted by predators.

* * *

During the rut, it's easy to overlook the rest of the Tetons' animals. Not only is the rut itself spectacular and diverting, but by the time the bulls are in full cry, many of the birds have split for the south, and the smaller mammals, such as ground squirrels and marmots, have begun to den up for the winter. Still, elk are only part of the scene, part of the rich and complex tapestry of interdependent plants and animals, which includes most of the species one usually associates with the wilder reaches of the Rockies: bears, mountain lions, bighorn sheep, free-ranging bison, moose, bald eagles, and many other creatures.

Like the plants, the Tetons' animals tend to distribute themselves among the park's major ecozones. Some, such as red squirrels and beavers, rarely stray from their preferred habitats. But others, such as elk, coyotes, and hawks, rove the entire park, crossing from zone to zone as needs change for food, reproduction, and protection.

The moist banks of the park's waterways brim with grasses, sedges, reedy plants, shrubs, and trees that offer animals food and protection from the weather and one another. Moose wade in the marshy backwaters, cropping aquatic plants and lifting their dripping heads to scan the shoreline. Yellow warblers, willow flycatchers, and western wood peewees dart from the foliage to snatch up insects swarming over the water. Belted kingfishers dive from their perches for minnows. Beavers ply the quiet waters, harvesting aspen and willow branches. Muskrats grub the muck for aquatic roots and tubers and are sometimes hunted by river otters. Leopard frogs bob stealthily among the cattails and often end their lives slipping down the gullets of great blue herons. Osprey swoop from the sky to yank trout and whitefish from their pools. And legions of mice, voles, chipmunks, ground squirrels, and other small mammals rustle through the underbrush, attracting coyotes, weasels, owls, marsh hawks, and other predators.

Next to ducks and geese, beavers are probably the most familiar wetland animals in the park. They live throughout the Tetons, building their dams and canals wherever water flows within convenient reach of the aspen trees and willow shrubs that yield their dietary staple—bark. Their ponds protect them from predators and ease the gathering of branches, which they cache on the bottom of the pool for winter consumption. The wetlands they create control erosion and furnish important habitat for waterfowl, various amphibians, and other mammals, including moose, muskrat, and otters. Familiar yet intriguing, these stout, trundling animals seem awkward on land, but they are beautifully adapted to life in the water. They have closeable nostrils, valves to shut their ears, lips that seal their mouths while chewing underwater, dense fur, streamlined bodies, and tails that act as rudders. They can submerge for fifteen minutes, thanks to a diving reflex that retards the heartbeat and diminishes blood

A trio of bull moose browse sagebrush—high in fat—on the floor of Jackson Hole. Moose spend the winter munching on willow twigs along the river-bottoms and nibbling on subalpine fir in the deep snow of mountain forests. Moose, the largest members of the deer family, can reach a weight of eighteen hundred pounds.

flow to the limbs, conserving oxygen.

River otters—sleek, playful, and intelligent—live along the banks of the Snake and are often seen in the canyon, where they scamper up on rocks and watch raftloads of tourists glide past. They also favor the park's marshes, backwaters, and sloughs. With their streamlined bodies, dense fur, webbed feet, large lungs, and long rudderlike tails, otters are as well-suited to life in the water as beavers. But because they are not much for digging, otters den in abandoned beaver lodges or vacant burrows dug by other animals.

Moose tend to summer in marshy areas, where their broad hooves keep them from sinking deeply into the muck while they tank up on aquatic plants rich in salt. These plants build up a reserve of sodium that carries moose through their low-salt winter diet of twigs, shrubs, and bark. Perfectly at ease in the water, moose wade through rivers and ponds, swim across lakes, and have been seen diving as deep as fifteen feet. In winter, their long legs allow them to high-step easily through deep snow in the subalpine forest.

Like elk, bull moose devote a tremendous amount of nutrients to the growth of antlers. Their racks are the most massive of any animal, reaching weights of seventy pounds and sometimes spanning six feet. Moose put their antlers to use primarily during the rutting season, which is as tough on bull moose as it is on elk. It's not uncommon for a bull moose to lose 40 percent of its body weight during an autumn of thrashing the vegetation, battling with competing males, and otherwise defending its territory. Unlike elk, however, moose are not harem breeders, and it is the female moose that bawls and moans and trolls the woods for a partner.

* * *

Deceptively monotonous, the sagebrush flats that extend across the floor of Jackson Hole teem with an abundance of small, timid creatures who spend their short lives under constant threat of attack. Deer mice born in the summer busily cache seeds for a winter that 95 percent of them will never see. If the owls don't get them, the weasels, foxes, and coyotes probably will. The same predators—along with hawks, falcons, and badgers—hunt the brush and grassy areas for ground squirrels, voles, shrews, and gophers. The heavy death toll requires a correspondingly high birth rate to stay ahead of predation. Some voles, for instance, are ready to breed three weeks after birth. Pronghorn, bison, mule deer, and elk also roam the sagebrush steppe. And in the spring, sage grouse males strut across their traditional mating sites, called "leks," where they pander to the ladies by spreading their tail feathers and vigorously undulating their inflatable chests.

Pronghorn, often called antelopes or just plain "goats" by locals, move across the floor of Jackson Hole in small herds. From a distance, a group in flight looks like a light brown smear gliding across the olive green landscape. Up close, they look like something off the African savannah—exotic in the extreme, with shiny black horns, enormous eyes, shaggy white rumps, and bands of cream and tan across their necks. Renowned for their speed, these

*S*hy, secretive, and rarely seen by people, cougars tend to hunt deer and elk, often waiting in a tree above a game trail and then dropping onto the backs of prey.

graceful animals can sprint for short distances at sixty miles per hour and cruise for at least four miles at a steady forty-five miles per hour. Running is their primary defense against predators, and their exceptionally keen vision (the equivalent of eight-power binoculars) gives them plenty of warning of impending danger.

Bison were reintroduced to Grand Teton in 1948, after park officials determined that they had been part of the area's traditional ecosystem. Today, about 160 bison roam the northern end of the valley. During summer, they wander into the eastern foothills and up into the southern reaches of Yellowstone Park. These immense animals, with their bulky forequarters, massive heads, enormous humps, and trim hindquarters, are the largest land animals in North America. A full-grown bull can weigh a ton and stand six feet at the shoulder. Cows are much smaller. During the rut, bulls posture and threaten one another. Their roars can be heard for miles, and their matches sometimes escalate into fights in which they ram heads and try to gore one another. Bison are dangerous even when their hormones aren't boiling over. Park visitors who underestimate the animal's temperament run the risk of being gored. Such incidents have become more and more common in the past few years.

Most of the deer in the Teton area are mule deer, though you'll occasionally see a white-tailed deer leaping gracefully through woodland areas on the west side of the range. Mule deer owe their name to their large, mulelike ears, which are a useful adaptation in open areas like the sagebrush flats and the grassy foothills, where faint sounds carry over long distances. Mulies browse mostly on evergreen twigs, saplings, and shrubs. Unlike white-tails, they tend to congregate in herds, the better to detect predators such as mountain lions. The smaller, more solitary white-tail sticks closely to a particular section of the forest, which it learns intimately—the sources of food and water, the potential dangers, and all the various escape routes. When alarmed, these deer lift their tails as if raising a white flag. Biologists think they do this to let a predator know it has been detected and that pursuit would be pointless.

Coyotes trot throughout the park, but they are most often seen on the floor of the valley. They have a well-deserved reputation for intelligence, cunning, and adaptability. For example, they often work ground squirrel burrows in pairs, with one coyote approaching in an obvious way to divert the squirrel's attention. Meanwhile, the second sneaks up from behind and ambushes the preoccupied rodent. They also follow badgers around. When the badger digs into a ground squirrel burrow, the coyote finds the scoot hole and pounces on any squirrel that makes a run for it. In other regions, wading coyotes have been seen bobbing for carp. They do not ordinarily hunt big game, but they happily feast on winter-killed elk and can be seen huddled around carcasses on the National Elk Refuge. Not in the least bit finicky, coyotes eat just about anything: rodents, rabbits, roadkill, birds, eggs, insects, snakes, fruit, nuts, turtles, frogs, crayfish, plants, even household pets.

Coyotes with a hankering for a sidedish of Rover sometimes hide while one of

Winter starvation is one of the few natural threats faced by adult bison, the largest land mammals in North America. The animals sweep their immense heads from side to side to clear snow from underlying forage. About 160 bison roam the northern portion of the park.

their number prances along the dog's rural lot line. When Rover gives chase, the coyote turns tail and leads the dog to the rest of the pack. It's usually the last time Rover gets asked out for dinner.

Except for black bears and the occasional white-tailed deer, few large animals inhabit the dense evergreen forests that blanket the east slopes of the Tetons. Elk, moose, and grizzly bears do move through from time to time, but most of the deep forest animals are smaller. Owls swoop silently between the branches. Woodpeckers, usually of the downy or hairy varieties, batter away at tree trunks. Porcupines gnaw on bark. Weasels bound after the ubiquitous mice, voles, and woodrats. Flying squirrels glide as far as 260 feet, maneuvering around tree trunks and executing ninety degree turns.

Red squirrels are perhaps the most familiar of the deep forest animals. Intelligent, aggressive, territorial in the extreme, they hurl abuse at all who intrude upon their domain. They eat mostly pine nuts but also invade bird nests to eat the eggs and young. Pine martens, large weasels, are one of the few predators agile and swift enough to chase red squirrels through the trees and kill them.

As for bears, until recently the conventional wisdom held that there weren't very many in the park's forests, and that the grizzlies lived only to the north along the outskirts of Yellowstone. However, during the especially dry summer of 1994, bear sightings of all kinds increased throughout the Teton area, as both blacks and grizzlies descended from the mountains in search of food. Grizzlies were seen as far south of Jackson as the Mosquito Creek drainage, and a sow with cubs strolled through the suburbs of South Park. Black bears hung around homes throughout the valley, and one even nosed its way into a house near Wilson by using the dog door. In normal years, though, the bears tend to avoid humans and are rarely seen anywhere but in the backcountry.

Though big and ponderous, these powerful animals are also fleet of foot. They can easily outrun a person, and they can keep pace with a horse over short distances. As predatory as they may seem, bears depend less on meat than on a wide variety of plants and insects. Grizzlies prey on young elk in the spring, and also bolt down the occasional ground squirrel, mouse, vole, or hunk of carrion. Black bears also hunt small mammals and will happily gnaw away on a rotting deer carcass. Mostly, though, both types of bears eat twigs, buds, berries, roots, grasses, sedges, and nuts. They also roll over stones and tear apart rotting stumps looking for insects and worms. Every autumn, they feast on huckleberries, which grow abundantly on the floor of lodgepole forests. This annual banquet not only fattens them up for a winter of hibernation, but it can also determine whether a female has cubs. Even if the sow has mated in the summer, her embryo may not attach to the uterine wall—unless she has gained enough weight to sustain herself and her cubs through the winter.

* * *

The ferocious climate that dominates the alpine region at the crest of the

Tetons presents animals with a formidable challenge. Many spend time there during the short summer—elk, bighorn sheep, grizzly bears, eagles, weasels, and coyotes, to name a few. They graze on wildflowers, grasses, and sedges, or hunt for marmots, ground squirrels, voles, and pocket gophers. But most animals retreat to lower climes as winter sets in. Those that remain cope with the bitter cold in various ways. Some hibernate. Others build up large caches of food. Weasels hunt all winter and stack in their dens the corpses of small rodents which they can devour at leisure.

Yellow-bellied marmots, which look very much like their close relative the groundhog, spend the summer waddling through the mountain meadows, munching on roots, berries, and wildflowers. Often seen sunning themselves on top of boulders, marmots dig their burrows at the edge of a meadow—under rocks and boulders that are too large for badgers and other predators to move. True hibernators, marmots accumulate fat all summer and then retreat to their burrows for the winter. In hibernation, a marmot's body temperature drops from ninety-five degrees to the mid-forties. Its heart rate slows from one hundred to fifteen beats a minute. Oxygen consumption drops to just 10 percent of normal, and it breathes just once every few minutes.

Pikas, those high-country hares about the size of a hamster, cannot hibernate. Instead, they spend the summer darting through the talus fields, cramming their tiny mouths with grass and other plants which they cure in stacks and then cache for the long winter.

Bighorn sheep spend their summers in the high country rambling among the cliffs, boulder fields, and meadows and grinding down mouthfuls of colorful wildflowers, grasses, and sedges. They gravitate toward the good forage available in open meadows but rarely stray very far from the security of rocky ledges and rugged terrain. Every autumn, the bigger rams engage in spectacular head-smacking duels to determine who will breed with receptive ewes. The collision is so forceful that rams have evolved a shock-resistant double cranium to absorb the impact. Even so, the blow can break the horns and skulls of smaller rams. Some sheep stay at high elevations during winter, but many descend to the flanks of the foothills, where winds blow forage clear of snow. Occasionally they even spend time on the floor of the valley. Mountain lions, coyotes, and bobcats all prey on sheep, and golden eagles attack lambs shortly after birth on the high, rocky ledges that are inaccessible to other predators.

* * *

Few of the park's animals are more apparent and active than birds. Some three hundred different species flit, flutter, soar, paddle, and wade throughout the Tetons. They include impressive raptors such as bald eagles, great gray owls, ospreys, and red-tailed hawks, as well as shorebirds, waterfowl, songbirds, woodpeckers, and flycatchers. Some are predators. Many are prey. A few are a little of both. They sport a stunning variety of colors and range in size from the tiny but fierce calliope hummingbird, whose wings vibrate at twenty to eighty beats per

second, to the magnificent and endangered trumpeter swan, whose wingspan reaches eight feet.

Hawks and other raptors are perhaps the easiest birds to spot. They circle high over the sagebrush flats and roost on roadside fence posts, sometimes with a limp rodent pinned under their talons. It takes patience or luck to see one of these birds take prey. I've waited an hour or more for a single red-tailed hawk to dive onto a prairie loaded with ground squirrels—only to see it come up empty-footed. Then again, I've stood with fly rod in hand, intent only on fishing, when an osprey slammed into the surface of Leigh Lake just a couple dozen yards away and carried off a fat cutthroat trout. I have never seen a peregrine falcon take a songbird in midflight, but it must be a riveting spectacle. The falcons can accelerate to more than 150 miles per hour as they dive for a bird and then strike it in a shower of feathers.

Perhaps my favorite birds, though, are ravens. Common, often dismissed as merely scavengers or pests, ravens are in fact wise, inventive birds, and I admire their savvy and audacity. For instance, they have been known to mug house cats. They'll wait for one to return home with a mouse, then rough up the cat and flap away with the rodent. They pirate kills in similar fashion from owls, otters, gyrfalcons, and gulls, but they also kill for themselves—sometimes in surprising ways. They are believed to hunt for rodents and rabbits and have been known to raid chicken coops. In Canada, small groups kill newborn reindeer. And in the Arctic, pairs have been seen killing baby seals: one cuts off the seal's retreat by guarding its hole in the ice while the other pecks at the seal's head.

It's not the killing that endears ravens to me. It's their craftiness, cunning, adaptability, and if you will, their open-mindedness. They seem more directly engaged in puzzling out the world around them than do most other birds, and they are always ready to try something new. Bernd Heinrich, in his wonderful book *Ravens in Winter*, describes how ravens on Mount Denali quickly learned that climbers marked food caches with bamboo stakes flying red flags. The birds would dig through at least three feet of snow to get at the boxes.

Just a few weeks ago, I saw a pair of adult ravens sitting on a wire with two of their young perched between them. They were watching cars go by. I suspect they were waiting for a ground squirrel to dart onto the road and cavort with a steel-belted radial. But in my more anthropomorphic moments, I wonder if the people driving the cars were not part of the lesson. What do ravens—or, for that matter, any of the park's higher animals—think about us? Are we simply a potential source of food? A danger? A nuisance? Perhaps there is a deeper understanding. When I hear a raven chuckle at me from a pine tree, I like to think so.

A *western version of the forest-dwelling white-tailed deer, mule deer live in more open and arid habitats. Their large ears are an adaptation to the roomier environment as is their tendency to gather in herds, the better to detect approaching predators.*

Pikas live among the talus fields of the Teton high country, darting among the rocks all summer to build up a cache of cured grasses and other plants that will see them through the winter.

Cougars—also called mountain lions or pumas—are highly adaptive and will roam from lowlands high into the mountains, wherever they find some woody cover and an abundant supply of prey, usually deer.

Mule deer generally stick to the sagebrush steppe and grassy foothills, where they browse on evergreen twigs, saplings, and shrubs.

In the spring, sage grouse males strut their tradition-al mating grounds, called "leks," suavely undulating their inflatable chests.

Bald eagles—also called American eagles—build massive nests and lay two to three eggs. They require large open spaces and waterways and feed almost wholly on fishes. Adult birds at least four years of age sport white heads and tail— their characteristic plumage.

and Douglas fir predominate along the lower slopes, but soon give way to subalpine forests of Engelmann spruce and subalpine fir. Woodpeckers, red squirrels, porcupines, and black bears are just a few of the many deep forest animals.

Above the trees sprawls the alpine zone, an expansive, boulder-studded landscape where hardy plants support just a handful of year-round residents such as the pika and the yellow-bellied marmot.

Rivers and streams cut throughout the park, forming lush ribbons of vegetation on the sagebrush flats, flowing slowly through sloughs and beaver ponds and supporting spongy mead-ows of wildflowers in the high country. River otters prowl the banks. Belted kingfishers dive for minnows, trout snap up mayflies, and moose munch on aquatic plants.

This compressed spectrum of life zones offers a scenic bargain. In a single day, you can hike through a range of habitats similar to what you'd encounter on a trip from the Great Plains to the Arctic Circle.

WILDLIFE HABITATS

Like so many areas in the Rocky Mountains, the Tetons compress an astonishing diversity of plants and animals into a relatively small area. A quick glance from the grass and sagebrush of the valley floor to the treeless crest of the range takes in a wide range of habitats, or life zones, each characterized by certain plant and animal species.

Ecologists recognize five major life zones. Starting from the floor of the valley, they include the sagebrush steppe, a dry, sometimes desertlike expanse of grass, sagebrush, and prairie wildflowers where hawks hunt for ground squirrels and pronghorn dash across the flats.

The rumpled foothills of the Gros Ventre Mountains enclose the east side of the valley. There, open slopes of grass and sagebrush alternate with groves of aspen and stands of Douglas fir and lodgepole pine.

On the other side of the valley, mountain forests blanket the east slopes of the Tetons. Lodgepole pine

Well-adapted to Jackson Hole's harsh winters, bison are unpredictable, surprisingly fleet of foot, and perfectly willing to charge and gore humans.

Black bears and grizzlies den up for the winter, but in summer the black bears tend to roam the dense evergreen forests while the grizzlies keep to the high country.

Although not found in the Tetons during the winter, Osprey spend their summers building huge nests of twigs and small branches, circling over Grand Teton's lakes and rivers and plunging now and then for trout and whitefish.

True hibernators, marmots dig their burrows at the edges of the park's mountain meadows and spend their summers fattening up on the season's wildflowers, roots, and berries.

A ny birdwatcher or student of Zen knows that if you want to find something badly enough, you must stop pursuing it. The harder you chase, the more elusive it becomes, whereas if you sit down, and wait, and listen, something is bound to happen.

I learned that lesson twenty years ago on a spring hiking trip in the Tetons. For three days I'd been tormented by the brilliant clear voice of an unseen bird. It was the loudest bird in the forest, calling from the high branches of conifers. I looked hard, thinking that any bird with such a voice box and such confidence in its song should be prominently visible. I expected a bird of some size, but after hours of actively chasing the calls through forest and meadow, I still hadn't caught a glimpse.

At last I gave up, and turned my attention to other things. That evening, as I crouched over a cooking fire, my eye was caught by a shadowy flicker of wings. Sitting on a pine twig no more than five feet away, a tiny gray bird launched into its now-familiar call: *chee-chee-chee-weechew-weechew-weechew-weechew-weeeet!* Then he tipped his head, showing off a bright red patch of feathers, and left me astonished. A ruby-crowned kinglet. A bird the size of my thumb with a voice that could fill the world.

Since then, every spring I listen for kinglets. For me, they mark the melting of snow. Whereas hermit thrushes, another voice of spring, begin their ethereal upward-spiral flutings while old snowbanks still lie wearily on the ground,

G ame trails criss-cross the woods throughout the park's forests. Sometimes the best way to see animals is not to follow a trail, but rather to sit quietly and wait.

STILL SITTING
LISTENING TO WILDERNESS

HARSH BEAUTY: ALPINE LAKES

Ringed by flower-packed meadows, filled with clear cold water, alpine lakes are the gems of the Teton high country. Their beauty belies their harshness, for few aquatic plants and animals manage to survive in them. Ice-bound well into July, their water temperatures rarely go much above forty degrees. Coming almost directly from melting snow fields and glaciers, the water is poor in nutrients and organic matter. During summer, intense high-altitude sunlight can damage algae and other plants, while in winter, ice and snow block the light.

Even so, their apparent sterility is deceptive. Alpine lakes are home to tiny organisms called nannoplankton, less than seventy-five microns in diameter and too small to cloud the water. Although invisible, they can play a role of major importance as food for slightly larger plankton, which in turn are eaten by insects and aquatic invertebrates including fairy shrimp and water fleas. Against all apparent odds, trout also thrive in some alpine lakes and grow to impressive sizes.

kinglets wait until yellow violets and spring beauties are in bloom. When I hear them, I know I can lie back in sun-warmed grass and listen and wait and see what comes along.

Still sitting. Sitting still. All that's required is to get away from the smells and sounds and confining perspectives of vehicles. You've got to walk, to put the dirt beneath your feet. Touch things. Sit on the ground. Get dusty. Smell the earth.

At the moment I am sitting with my back against a boulder in Cascade Canyon: hiker recumbent. The kinglets are singing, and spring is popping. I came here to take inventory of the season. It is time for moose calves and the first blooms of balsamroot. There should be puffballs and morels poking through the newly thawed earth, and the potent shoots of emerging skunk cabbage. I walked for a while, checked the meadows for moose or other large animals, found none, and then settled down beside this boulder to wait for whatever might happen along.

I came here for the very reasons that make Cascade Canyon one of the park's most popular short hiking destinations. On the west side of Jenny Lake, it occupies the scenic heart of the Tetons—the Cathedral Group on one side, Mounts St. John and Moran on the other. Unlike most Teton canyons, this one climbs gradually into the range. In fact, it provides a relatively easy route through the mountains to the western side, making it the most welcoming of the park's spectacular hiking routes.

I did not get an early start, which meant that I joined a full boatload of other nature lovers on the ride across Jenny Lake. Disembarking on the far shore, we filed past thirty or forty people waiting to board the return boat. The trail, six feet wide in places, is the Teton equivalent of a freeway and is popular for good reason. All the essential elements of the Tetons are found along this route—the morainal lake, cliffs soaring up from the western shore, glaciers hanging below the lofty peaks, a stream cascading beside the trail, a superb waterfall, deep forest, open meadows, assorted wildlife, and a prominent viewpoint overlooking the valley.

It would not seem a likely place to find solitude in midday, but find it I have. I walked about a half mile beyond Inspiration Point on a gently rolling trail through meadows and conifer groves until at random I turned off and made my way over glacially smoothed granite to this sitting place. No one else here. Complete privacy, but not silence.

Branches clatter. Twigs crack. Things go thump. Insect wings whine. Pine squirrels chitter. The day is calm, but occasional gusts of wind move down from crags, sighing through the trees, bringing riffs of water song from Cascade Creek. A black bumblebee drones past like a prototypical blimp and sets me to wondering why an insect only an inch long should seem huge while a kinglet four times as big seems tiny. Flying overhead, a pair of Clark's nutcrackers make juvenile delinquent screeches. From somewhere back in the spruce shadows comes the deep, thumping tractor sound of a ruffed grouse drumming, drumming.

Marmots are out after their long hibernation. One climbs a boulder nearby and, catching sight of me, spends a few hyperactive minutes barking a warning to the rest of the world. There's a snowshoe rabbit at the edge of the meadow, its coat still in transition between winter white and summer gray. Finally the marmot is satisfied, falls silent, and climbs down from its perch. In the relative peace, I am able to hear a rustling in the dry grass near my foot. A vole makes nervous forays into the sunlight, then disappears. But even then I can trace its progress by the shiver of plant stems, and occasionally I catch a glimpse of shadowy gray fur. Some predatorial instinct urges me to make a grab for it. If I were a coyote, this would be like watching a blueberry muffin browning in the oven. Turning my attention to smaller things, I realize that the ground is busy with insects. Among them, I notice a dead leaf moving, apparently of its own volition. Bending close, I can hear a faint crackling sound as the leaf scratches against others. I pick it up and find an earthworm gallumphing recklessly along. I have read that when robins on the lawn cock their heads, they are actually listening for earthworms, but I never expected to hear one myself.

Without sitting still, you might never realize how noisy it is out there in the peace and quiet.

* * *

The same gentle occupation can be carried out with great effect from a canoe. One of the best places in the park is Oxbow Bend on the Snake River below Jackson Lake. If you've driven west from Moran Junction, you know this place. It swings a scenic, psychic sledgehammer: Mount Moran thrusting above its reflected image, quiet waters cut by the gentle ripples of cruising trumpeter swans. Most visitors stop wide-eyed for a photograph. They leave with an indestructible memory.

One summer day we made a family trip of it—my wife, Wendy, piloted the canoe from the stern so I could sit idle in the bow making occasional motions with a fly rod; our two-year-old daughter, Kestrel, rode eagerly amidships.

The current carried us slowly. We let it take us where it wanted, which at one point was a backwater occupied by a beaver lodge. Naturally, we looked for beavers but instead found that a family of river otters had moved in. Heads bobbing above the surface, five of the sleek mammals emerged to investigate us, swimming beneath the canoe, popping up at random like figures in a carnival game, all to K's enormous delight. And ours. Farther along, we thought we saw them again, until they dove, slapping their flat tails on the surface, and we knew that this time we had found the real beavers. Gazing over the side, we could see squads of suckers—native bottom-feeding fish—patrolling the gravel bottoms, along with trout and whitefish swifting through the long, waving underwater forests. I let my line sink, trailing a nymph deep underwater, and caught an eighteen-inch cutthroat; K touched its namesake red slash before we slipped it back into the river and watched it shoot back beneath the waving green canopy. Around one corner, we came upon a young bull moose standing shoulder deep,

Fog rises from Oxbow Bend, a quiet corner of the park. It's a good place for drifting in a canoe and watching beaver, moose, river otters, and great blue herons go about their daily routines.

RANCHING THE TETONS

"Being adventuresome," wrote Francis Judge of her pioneer grandmother, "she made her way to the wild, remote Jackson Hole country. Here with John Shive [her husband] she found her paradise. They and the West were young together, rough and unbounded."

Ranching began at the base of the Tetons in the 1880s when Mormon settlers, driven from their Utah land by a persistent drought, forced their wagons over roadless Teton Pass. They were looking for better conditions; what they found was hard beauty, a place where gardening required the patience of Job, and farming was impossible. Ranching became their way of life, and even that was never easy. Suffering from the Great Depression, many ranchers willingly sold out in the 1930s to agents of John D. Rockefeller, whose intention was to consolidate the valley's private land and donate it—33,562 acres— to the public as part of a national park. Despite fierce local opposition and complaints about heavy-handed eastern money, he accomplished his goal when the park was established in 1950. Some of the old ranch buildings survive, along with a number of Jackson Hole ranches that remain privately owned. Hereford cows, buckrail fences, and irrigated hay meadows are still an important part of the Teton scene.

dipping his head underwater to pull up succulent aquatic plants, watching us placidly as he chewed. My notes from that day record ospreys, cormorants, mergansers, a red-tailed hawk, a bald eagle, a heron, two pelicans. Presiding over it all, Mount Moran in its summer glory.

There is so much to be said about the Snake River. Rising from the Teton Wilderness, it flows through elk-filled meadows along the southern edge of Yellowstone National Park, winds its way past high grizzlied ridges and through dark stands of conifers. Its clear waters polish the native stones, flow through the gills of cutthroat trout, slide beneath arches of overhanging meadow grass, and do this almost entirely unseen by human eyes until it rounds the curve opposite the ranger station at Yellowstone's south entrance. A few miles farther south, where it crosses the boundary of Grand Teton National Park, the Snake is as wild a river as the continent can still claim.

But not for long. Even within the national park's protective boundaries, the Snake is a kept current—owned, measured, packaged, and delivered. Jackson Lake was originally a smaller but natural body of water. The Jackson Lake Dam, built in 1907 before the park was created, put a harness on the river and raised the lake level thirty-seven feet, turning it into a storage facility to meet demands of irrigation, hydro-generation, recreational activities, trout and salmon management, flood control, and more.

The Snake once ebbed and flowed with the seasons. In spring flood, it poured clear and icy from the lake, spilling over its banks, pushing through the cottonwoods, scouring new channels, and sweeping its bed clear of debris. The river still pushes out clear and icy from Jackson Lake, but now it comes from under the dam at controlled levels determined by snow surveys, long-range weather predictions, the state of downstream reservoirs, and the ebb and flow of politics. Cleansing floods are prohibited. Silt covers the gravel beds where trout used to spawn, and deadfall piles up in the braided channels.

Below the park, the Snake comes under jurisdiction of the U.S. Army, whose Corps of Engineers maintains a series of dikes designed to prevent the river from doing what it naturally would do, and what it surely some day will do again—meander back and forth across its two-mile-wide floodplain, now the preferred building site for ten-thousand-square-foot log cabins. Water hates to flow in a straight line. Rivers bend naturally, attempting to carve bends with a radius twice their width. Confronted by militarily precise dikes, the water fights to regain a natural course.

Some day it will succeed (perhaps helped by the next Teton Fault earthquake), and there will be a lot of expensive cowboy furniture floating with the driftwood toward Idaho. In the meantime, few people notice the river's altered nature, and it seems that most plants and animals are unaffected by the dam. The illusion of wildness—if not the reality—remains intact, especially in the stretch below the Buffalo Fork Junction, the section called by river outfitters the "scenic float." Here the river gathers speed and challenges even experienced boaters. For that stretch I prefer a raft over a canoe. I want the stability of a wide boat. There are no rapids to speak of, no white-water waves, but plenty of rapidly moving water hurling itself from bank to bank, splitting itself around islands, then coming back together, always in a hurry, always capable of surprises.

Mostly I watch for log jams; if you take the wrong channel, you can be swept into a deadly tangle of driftwood—deadly because boats tend to broach against the driftwood, spilling passengers who are then pulled into the tangle and held underwater by the powerful current. Every few years someone makes a mistake and dies that way. But there are other surprises. One autumn afternoon I took the raft on the stretch from Buffalo Fork to Deadman's Bar. It was one of those perfect, azure-sky, Indian summer days. My thoughts had drifted elsewhere when, speeding along beneath a steep cutbank, I looked up to see a bull bison lumber to the grassy edge, ten feet above the water. He halted in a cloud of dust. His abrupt appearance suggested danger. What was he up to? There was no place to hide and nothing I could do with the boat. The current was taking me directly under him. He hung overhead darkly like a thundercloud as I drifted past without incident. Yet something in his eye made me think my rush of fear was not pure foolishness.

Farther downstream, the sound of elk bugling drew me to shore. I tied the boat and walked back among the towering, leafless cottonwoods. Moving carefully, I worked my way into the midst of the herd. I could smell the powerful rankness of the bulls and feel the excitement of the cows. I stood still, inconspicuously, and they ignored me. They knew I was there but I was irrelevant. The sun slid behind the mountains, taking the day's thin warmth with it. In its place came cold ground fog, in which the trees stood like calligraphy and elk moved like ghosts, frosty grass crackling beneath their hooves. I stayed until twilight, completely absorbed, until two great horned owls began hooting in the gloom. Back at the raft, the river was breathing a chill mist. Ice had gathered in the oarlocks. Shivering from cold—and from nervousness about rowing in the dark—I pushed off. Before long, stars were out and the river was as black as a grave. After several miles, I was absurdly grateful to see the boat landing, and I knew I had been pushing the season for sitting still.

* * *

But here it is spring again. Once more the days are long. I'm sitting with my back against a boulder in Cascade Canyon. Having lost interest in voles and earthworms, my mind wanders.

I am watching wispy spring clouds play among the crags of Teewinot Mountain when I hear a quiet footfall to my left, over my shoulder. Not all that quiet—something heavy is moving toward me. Trying not to spook whatever it is, I turn my head in slow motion and see a moose calf thirty feet away. Nearly newborn. Cute little guy on oversized legs, reddish brown fur, jerky movements of his curious head . . . but where is his mother? I can't see her, and the thought makes me nervous. I know how protective moose mothers can be. I've seen them threaten coyotes and dogs, and one cold winter day a moose dam kept me in my house for several hours. Her calf of that year, a big capable animal in his own right, had bedded down on my front deck. Every time I opened the door to come out, she trotted menacingly in my direction. Junior watched with what I took to be the glee of a juvenile delinquent: "Get 'im, Ma!" And I was right to stay inside. When the two of them finally left, the calf grazed the side of my car, shearing off a rearview mirror.

I consider waving my arms, shooing the youngster away, scaring him, until I hear another sound over my right shoulder. Heart pounding now, I turn my head with less control and more speed. There she is, as yet unalarmed, unaware of me. Grazing. She looks as lean and hard as a race horse. I freeze as her head comes up. She checks her precious offspring, then goes back to grazing.

I'm caught between them, sitting on my butt. She could break me against this rock like a stepped-on bug. A few minutes ago, this meadow seemed so tame, so unthreatening. Now this. Perhaps, I hope, they will continue on past. I'm encouraged to see that the calf is moving faster than his mother.

No chance. She senses me. Smells me, I suppose. Her ungainly dinosaur head comes up in a rush of hormones, her ears swivelling, searching, still unsure of what I am.

I mean her no harm. I could do her no harm. I could do her calf no harm, but she doesn't know that. Half a ton of bristling suspicion, she regards me as potential danger. She advances a stride. I think I'm about to get the crap beat out of me. She snorts, a low snuffling whoof like she's trying to clear her nose of a bad odor. I tense against the unsympathetic rock. It pushes back. The moose comes a step closer, now only about twenty feet away, her head low, radar locked in. I've lost track of the calf. I'm staring at the cow trying not to blink, wondering if there's any way to scoot around the boulder if she makes another move. If I jump, how will she react? I have to do something, but what? I feel like a rabbit frozen in the headlights.

Time passes. A minute. Two. Three, I don't know. But I can barely stand it. I'm about to turn chicken and do something, maybe start yelling and flapping my arms, when there comes a noise from the edge of the meadow. The calf has made a startled movement, and suddenly the world is in motion. The mother's head swings. Her body wheels. I straighten my legs and vault backward over the rock. The moose thunders by on her way to defend the calf. I scramble for the protection of trees, and when I get a chance to look back she's strutting around on the far side of the meadow, motherly defense mechanisms on full alert, attention focused into the forest, away from me.

Now it's the calf who's staring in my direction. Easy boy. Don't tell your mom. I melt into the trees a few paces, then walk backwards for several hundred yards. There are times when still-sitting can result in encounters too close for comfort.

ACKNOWLEDGMENTS

A book is never the work of a single person, a single pen. In writing this one we relied on many others for enlightenment, encouragement, correction, and corroboration. Many thanks to the park naturalists who do such a fine job of interpreting Grand Teton's wonders for so little pay; to Sharlene Milligan and the Grand Teton Natural History Association for their enthusiasm for this project from the outset and for their willingness to read, offer helpful suggestions, and keep us from putting our foot in a fresh one.

Of the many books we found useful, we'd like to mention and recommend these: *For Everything There is a Season* by Frank Craighead; *Mountains and Plains, The Ecology of Wyoming Landscapes* by Dennis H. Knight; *Land Above the Trees* by Ann Zwinger and Beatrice Willard; *Birds of Grand Teton National Park* by Bert Raynes; *The Birder's Handbook* by Paul Erlich et alia; Mountain Press's excellent series of roadside geology guides; *Creation of the Teton Landscape* by David Love and John Reed; *A Fieldguide to Rocky Mountain Wildflowers* by John and Frank Craighead and Ray Davis; and *The Sex Life of Plants* by Alec Bristow.

We'd also like to thank our parents, Karl and Joan, for getting this little collaboration of brothers going in the first place, and for pointing our noses, feet, and hearts into the woods.

JEREMY SCHMIDT
Jackson, Wyoming

THOMAS SCHMIDT
Victor, Idaho

A *grove of aspens stands along the edge of a Teton meadow— one of many quiet corners of the park.*

INDEX

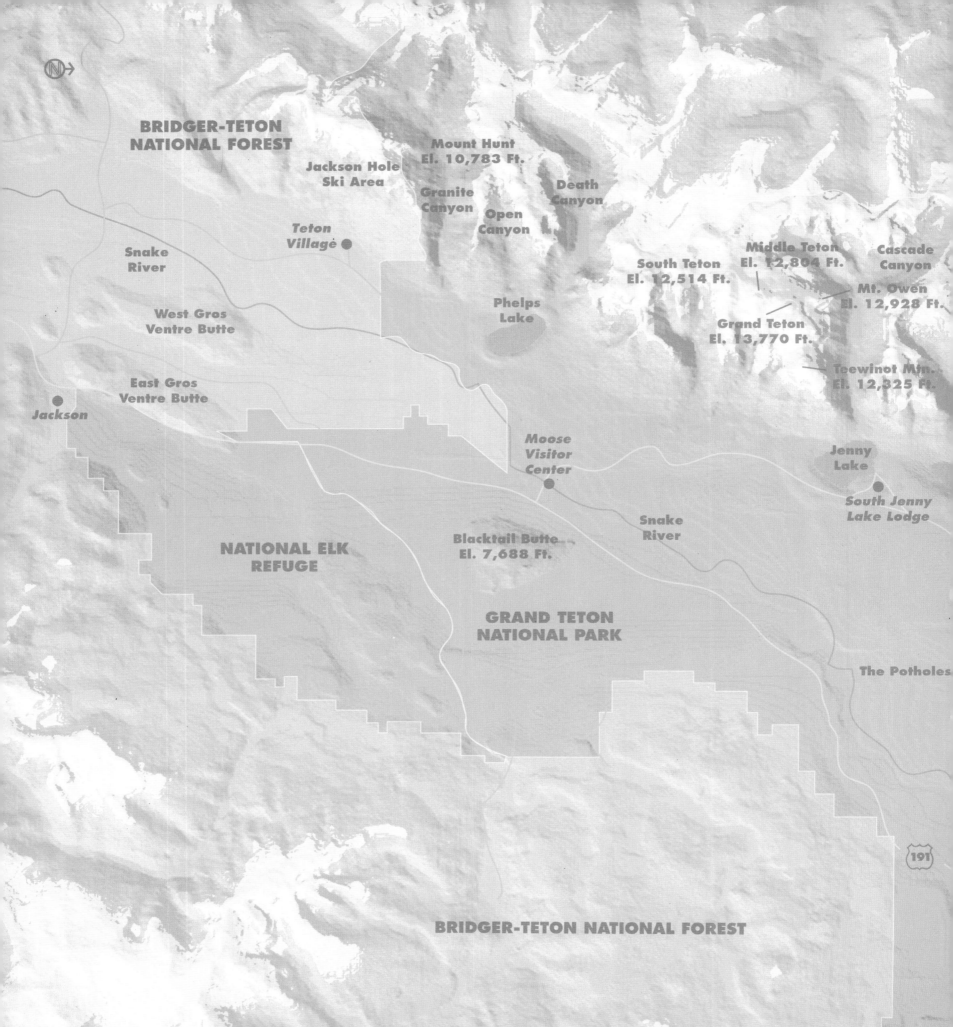